WISDOM
EXPOSED

WISDOM EXPOSED

RA-SHIEKE BOYD

ATRU PATH PUBLISHING

ATRU PATH PUBLISHING
NEW YORK, NY, UNITED STATES
www.atrupathpublishing.com

WISDOM EXPOSED

Ra-shieke Boyd

Library of Congress Control Number: 2023909154

ISBN: 979-8-218-20457-0

For information about special discounts for bulk purchases, please contact Atrupath Publishing.

Author: Ra-shieke Boyd
Cover design: Ra-shieke Boyd

To my wonderful and amazing wife Selma, whose love, devotion, and support have been constants throughout my journey, even in the face of the most demanding challenges. May my success in all of my endeavors highlight and reflect your faith in me. I love you for all of eternity.
Thank you.

You must not wait on others or blame outside circumstances. It is your responsibility to seek out your purpose, education, and prosperity. It is you who must perceive, prepare for, and create opportunities.

- Ra-shieke Boyd

Contents

INTRODUCTION

Wisdom is substantially a subject of divine enlightenment, nobility, the ability to perceive the many events of life, and applying one's judgment to assess situations prudently before or as they arise. When reflecting on the topic of wisdom, some may say that it requires enduring numerous ordeals and amassing a vast and profound compilation of knowledge and transformative experiences through various endeavors in life. Nonetheless, wisdom is attained by astutely observing the circumstances and events of life, cultivating exceptional principles, and not succumbing to the influence or deception of those who themselves have been led astray, enslaved by ignorance, or surrendered to immorality.

The powerful ideals within this book provide us with simple yet profound expressions of inspiration, emphasizing the crucial importance of cultivating high self-esteem while enabling us to analyze the various aspects of life from a positive and constructive resolve. By tracing the consequences of these realities in our own lives as well as the lives of others, we can acquire the necessary tools and knowledge to navigate every challenge with grace and prudence. In doing so, we can enhance the value of our life experiences, enabling us to seize advantageous opportunities for success, fulfillment, and personal growth.

To maximize the multitude of revelations that are unveiled as you study the passages of Wisdom Exposed, you should develop an earnest appreciation for the edifying expressions and intrinsic value of their divine commission. This commission of enlightenment is an ideal guide for those seeking to make the world a place where knowledge, divine order, prosperity, and morality are thoroughly instilled in the mind and spirit of every living being. For those who are truly wise desires for everyone who has life to enjoy and appreciate it, for every sensible creature to have the right to a healthy environment, to enjoy the grace of nature in all its vast creations, and to do so without the callous hands and ravenous deeds of ignorant men and women disturbing or destroying their state of peace, or quality of their homes.

If this invaluable guide is not widely disseminated, humanity will continue to experience failure and undue hardship, remaining disconcerted and unable to attain the success of divinity they truly deserve. Therefore, it's crucial that we make this knowledge available to the masses so that we can make informed choices about life and avoid the repeated consequences of ignorance. Those who fail to perceive and internalize the powerful truths put forward in these pages risk missing the path of prosperity and falling victim to the crippling effects of adversity.

As you delve into the enlightened passages of Wisdom Exposed, you will discover a groundbreaking treatise on the pervasive impact of perception, prudence, totality, and your innate divinity. This much-needed exploration offers an innovative perspective, shedding light on essential aspects of the human experience and providing insights that are both profound and practical. The ultimate goal of this literary masterpiece is to inspire powerful ideals in the mind of any person who aspires to lead a noble and exceptional life dedicated to constructing and maintaining an independent state of unencumbered sovereignty.

It must be understood that the author encourages and signifies the importance of nobility with the intention of instilling prudence, unadulterated ideals, and a gratifying lifestyle into the spirit of his readers. Moreover, it is imperative that you

INTRODUCTION

comprehend the author's perspective regarding this compilation as a matter of conformity, progression, and high esteem for every man, woman, and maturing youth. The overarching ideals of Wisdom Exposed are founded on the notion of elevating the essence of virtue in life, and making life more meaningful, purposeful, and abundant for everyone. This is the author's paramount objective, as it ought to be for all who aspire to refine the stature and conventional ideals of humanity.

This literary gem is bound to captivate and enthrall anyone seeking to attain the benefits of an autonomous state and possessing a fervent desire to become a purveyor of wisdom's arcane secrets. Divided into twelve sections, each containing 50 proverbs, this anthology is designed for ease of use. Comprising more than 500 proverbs, it is intended to be not just read, but pondered and deeply ingrained. I implore you not to merely peruse these proverbs, but to contemplate each one earnestly before proceeding to the next, absorbing and applying their significance to any circumstance that may prove applicable and valuable to the course of your life.

Those who ascend the lofty ladder of wisdom are bestowed a plethora of rewarding experiences, and their every endeavor shall be crowned with exceptional achievements. Acquire a deep understanding of the significance of wisdom, and in return, you will receive blessings instead of misfortune and establish yourself in the impregnable sanctuary of enlightenment.

-- Immerse yourself in the treasure trove of knowledge presented in this book, for the wisdom you acquire will invigorate your zeal to explore and unearth the esoteric doctrines and mystical teachings of the divine and sagacious masters.

Commit to your purpose, wear the crown.

EXPOSED

I

SECTION ONE

Wisdom Exposed

The master was asked, "Who taught you?"
He answered, "No one taught me. I saw that the ignorance of
the fool was shameful, so I avoided it."

- Ancient Scripture

1. You are the center of the universe, an indispensable and distinct being of life! Much like the sun or a perpetual source of clean water, you are unequivocally essential. With enlightenment and determination, you may unlock and possess the power of divinity.

2. Faith serves as the spiritual stimulus that empowers you to exercise your capacity to believe and accomplish any feat. The divine components of faith comprise sincere conviction, dependable knowledge, earnest pursuit, unflinching exertion, proficiency, anticipation, and inevitable fruition.

3. Without deep concentration, excessive pains, strong discipline, focused endurance, faith-filled endeavors, and constant work, one cannot grow stronger or become wiser. Embrace the challenges ahead with open arms, and let your unyielding determination guide you towards the illimitable potential that awaits.

4. Those who make discipline rule over pleasure and the pursuit of knowledge greater than idleness are on a path affluent with success. They will succeed.

5. Temptation is initiated upon the feebleminded and leads astray all who lack self-discipline and contentment. Strengthen your will to excel beyond every weakness.

6. The wise attach little importance to lofty positions in society, and no offer of wealth or power can compel them to act immorally.

7. Desire and you devise a quest. Before advancing, be certain what you are pursuing is worth the time, effort, and energy you will consume in your pursuit and realize the work that must be completed to attain or fulfill your desire.

8. Make yourself a requisite faculty to all that will manifest the realities you desire and learn to employ and commission all things. Whatever you speak or do in faith shall be realized.

9. It is better to keep quiet and have people think you're a fool than to open your mouth and remove all doubt. The wise speak because they have something intelligent to say, however, fools speak because they need something to do and have not discovered the benefits of intellect or the many important feats that require their immediate and undivided attention.

10. Some are inclined to engage in matters of great importance to sustain the order, well-being, and provisions of many while

others indulge and are concerned only with their own personal desires.

11. To live with purpose, advance in understanding, and grow in faith are the zeal and strength of the soul. When matured these create dynamics in the mind so powerful even the thriving forces of nature may not prevail against them.

12. Comprehension is the paramount of all universal attributes and reigns supreme over all things. Nothing is more essential than the great ability to acquire and apply knowledge.

13. It is not wise to judge with partial awareness. Instead one should gain an absolute understanding of the subject at hand so that he or she will not be considered ignorant or experience the effects of error.

14. What appears simple or obvious may be more complex or puzzling than what is perceived. The wise will never assume, underestimate, or judge solely on what is revealed; there may be hidden realities that are cleverly disguised.

15. Many concepts and material objects will be presented to you. Be wise and know that many of them are unacceptable.

16. Withdraw from or remove anything that is harmful or may be preventing you from achieving your goal. Devise order and keep your path straight, clear, and firm.

17. Foreseeing the potential challenges that may arise in life is a vital skill, one that can only be attained by acquiring knowledge and insight. Those who lack such foresight are vulnerable to the forces that may come upon them, while those who possess it have the ability to anticipate, prepare for, and overcome any obstacle that arises.

18. The many concepts and entities which empower and sustain reality are all pieces to the puzzle known as life. It is

your objective to learn, order, and bring them together to construct the actual essence of life as you envision and desire to experience it.

19. Sin is the root of a distorted mind and destroys the innocence and moral quality of one's character. You must be pure and holy in all your ways living your whole life with high standards and integrity.

20. Many things are disclosed, and many things are not revealed.

21. There is a quest that you alone must transverse and although there will be others to accompany you from time to time or from one path to the next, no one will be with you at every turn of your course. Take wisdom with you wherever you go and your journey will be much more manageable and advantageous.

22. With the power of thought and observation you will mentally and emotionally respond to everything you acknowledge and focus on. Be cautious with what you concern yourself with and consider how you must deal with everything you give attention to.

23. You are entirely the master of your deeds, the commander of your actions, the model of your beliefs, the constructor of your conditions, and the author of your destiny. Ignorantly or intelligently you will develop and evolve according to the way you perceive and mentally resolve every issue and situation presented to you.

24. It is wiser to build and live in conditions you desire to inhabit than to find yourself stagnant and confined to undesirable standards and conditions established by others. Secure your essence by forging upon reality a status and environmental setting that suits you.

25. By changing doubt into enthusiastic faith you may change adversity into prosperity. Do this and you may triumph and achieve whatever it is you wish to pursue.

26. A trend stirs and enthralls many to embrace perverse concepts or fall victim to the alluring force of materialism. However, those who are content are unmoved and accept and acquire only what is required and necessary.

27. Family and friends are the most cherished and invaluable treasures of life. Their worth surpasses that of any material possession and they should be treated with the utmost reverence and care. Cherish them as the true gifts of life, and relish the moments spent with them through meaningful actions and heartfelt deeds.

28. When giving counsel be sure you can tolerate and endure the suggested advice of what you tell others to do. Any advice you give should be positive and beneficial to the good of those you counsel.

29. Appearance and demeanor give great evidence to many variations of one's character. Therefore, establish yourself with the qualities of cleanliness, godly standards, and respectable conduct.

30. What you seek isn't always found where you believe it may be attained, and what you attain isn't always what you truly desire.

31. By tracing the effects of every action you may receive the wit of circumspection and foreknowledge.

32. Only a simpleton repeats deeds that produce harmful, futile, or negative results. However, the wise apply their efforts only to that which prove beneficial to their health and prosperity.

33. It is not your physical essence that they are truly attentive to but your actions and response to their actions. You are reputed by those who are aware of your actions, habits, conduct, and character.

34. The cause of suffering comes from the lack of knowledge, a yearning for unfulfilled desires, or the loss of someone or something cherished.

35. Pursue those things you desire only when you are competent and wise enough to possess them responsibly.

36. Wisdom is the fount of knowledge, order, and manifestation. However, ignorance and fatuity pollutes a pure and wholesome source.

37. It is not money that makes people fortunate, wealthy, extremely successful, or happy, but rather the application of exceptional thoughts and productive endeavors. It is wise to understand that thought activates actions which in turn actualize the events of reality.

38. Every soul possesses its own unique characteristics, mysteries, and interpretations of concepts. You are at liberty to inquire, encounter, and judge the essence of any conscious being at your own risk. Be wise not to succumb to anyone that will affect you with immoral ideas or foul habits.

39. One creates one's success out of the same opportunities in which others experience defeat. The results differ with one's intellectual capacity to fathom and perceive with correctness and the benefit or lack of one's ability to acquire knowledge, innovate, and administer accurate application.

40. Make way for those who are relentlessly purposeful and valorously determined, or be prepared to halt them with the same irrepressible impulse.

41. As a stream tours its course through the mountains flowing sometimes gently and peacefully and at others moving turbulently through rushing rapids, so everyone living must encounter various events.

42. By your habits, thoughts, and actions you will find yourself accompanied by those with similar characteristics, mentalities, and situations. You will attract or be drawn to those who in some way harmonize with your philosophies of life. Whether you realize these characteristics or not, they are present.

43. It is not the idle and feeble-minded who are truly a threat or danger, but those who are intelligent, overly ambitious, and striving for power and dominance who you should be cautious of.

44. To struggle is an opportunity to acquire and develop those essential skills and qualities that would lay dormant without the pains of trial and error. One must strive to develop his or her knowledge, status, and illimitable abilities.

45. Those without faith credits opportune occurrences as coincidence. However, those who have faith acknowledge these aligned events as the results of applicative efforts and anticipated occurrences achieving their expectancy.

46. The power of suggestion alone can create favorable circumstances or cause disastrous eventualities. Caution your mind to remember this truth.

47. To live is to possess observance, to prevent affliction and perpetuate prosperity is the supreme benefit of intelligence.

48. Hope pursues, adamant faith prevails. Where there is true faith there will be continuance and achievement.

49. True educators are vastly more concerned with the intellect than the disparity of those entrusted to them and focus predominantly on one's capability and desire to learn.

50. A lackadaisical person receives trumpery things, but a person of high quality and true diligence acquires things of great value.

II

SECTION TWO

1. New situations create opportunities for those who are able to assess their perception of these events with prudence. It is essential to develop constructive ideas in every situation to maximize your potential.

2. Knowledge yields many resources, provisions, and advantageous opportunities. The more you retain the more access you will have to administer your will effectively to control the conditions and circumstances of your life.

3. The eyes may lead you astray, therefore it is better to perceive with your mind. This way you are mentally focused on the objective and status you've envisioned and desire to achieve, and nothing will cause you to deviate from your path.

4. The accumulation of wisdom is like using a cup to draw water from a stream that flows perpetually, there will always be more than one can consume. However, even these small portions are sufficient to infuse one's intellect to achieve greater depths of enlightenment.

5. Thorough and accurate preparation reveals the efforts of faithful anticipation. Those who proceed in this manner will acquire the abilities of leadership, foreknowledge, and the consistency of achievements.

6. Keen and active participation is the most effective method for learning and experience your most proficient teacher. Pursue wisdom in everything so you may absorb every advantageous subject with the assurance of their enduring purposes.

7. It is the eminent responsibility of every wise adult to instill knowledge, morality, confidence, faith, and wisdom into the mind of every child. By doing this, no one will have to endure the blame of failure, for the children will develop, succeed, and prosper long into their adulthood and many generations thereafter.

8. The perspective of any event can be for one an unpleasant experience and for another a desirable incident.

9. There are times you will have to think for others perceiving both what they perceive and what they do not perceive.

10. The choices you make will lay a path for the circumstances you will encounter throughout your life. Therefore, you should give great consideration to the destiny you wish to realize and consider what you must do to achieve it. Be wise and prudent with the course of your future prospects.

11. Initially you are placed in circumstances and conditions that are beyond your ability to evade or gain control over. However, if you inquire to understand the realities surrounding your being you may become an influential force in many events and gain the knowledge, power, and abilities necessary to advance your status, position, and opportunities.

12. When a productive and successful person or entity is progressing it is wise of you to get involved using whatever resources, abilities, and talents you have to prevail with the development of every positive achievement. The objective of success is to increase your knowledge, awareness, and accessibility.

13. From within one seeks outwardly. Perceive what it is you seek outwardly, and you may come to know what you are within.

14. Be the person you choose to be, but it is wise to remember you are always on display and recalled by your actions and reputation.

15. Like a sea turtle from its eggshell into the vast mysteries of the sea, so is every experience encountered by every living soul; a journey filled with the unknown probabilities of success, failure, and all the obstacles and elements that exist within the events of life.

16. Those who are truly dexterous and masterful do not need to hope, doubt, or worry that they may fail. For they are extensively engaged in the practice of their abilities and exceptionally competent with the use of their faculties. Competence demonstrates the dexterity of one's knowledge, abilities, intellectual or physical capacity to employ those abilities, and one's wisdom and faith to control any situation within the scope of those adroit abilities.

17. The purpose of an education is to become knowledgeable, resourceful, competent and to enhance your ability to prosper. Regardless of how much you've acquired, there is always much more to be attained.

18. The mind is both telescopic and microscopic. When used accurately one may observe those things that are too remote or too near for those whose eyes and ears are inattentive. Only

those who are earnestly attentive may perceive, comprehend and accomplish what others may not.

19. The ideas of life and the universe exist precisely in the mind. Understand this and you will realize your essential purpose is to acquire and retain information, impart reason to your conceptual perspective of that information, infer that information to accord with your purpose, and use those concepts to acquire and create the entities and sources that will be conducive to your existence.

20. Be convinced of this; the mind may devise and accomplish whatever its intellectual capacity attributes to accurate application. As a conscious force of the universe, you are bound solely by the extent of your knowledge and passion to acquire the abilities and entities necessary to carry out your objective.

21. It is wiser to test a system by what it fails to achieve rather than its strong and thriving faculties. Acknowledge this truth and you may increase the strength and quality of any entity or established order.

22. Those with an intensified aim may advance through any obstacle and acquire the efforts of others to perform in accord with their purpose. However, those who are unprepared, hesitant, or indecisive will be hindered by many opposing forces and obstacles that would not dare enter the path of those who are vehemently determined.

23. Your time is your most valuable asset and what you do with it is the most important decision you will make. You must invest your time performing those tasks that will give you a life of stability and comfort and attain the best quality of all the things you desire as quickly as possible.

24. Reality is revealed in the ever-fleeting moments of now. As each of these moments passes, all that exists in them are miraculously disposed of leaving nothing more than

inconsistent residue of the translucent memories of those who witness the event, and if there was no one to witness, these events will go forever concealed from their successors.

25. Once you've experienced or perceived the true effects of any action or event you must determine whether they were beneficial, productive, healthy, moral, harmful, or demoralizing. Consider whether you should accept and allow those actions or events to recur.

26. Many things are natural in their being and many things are conceptually implied. Evaluate your beliefs and consider all realities. Things may not be as they are generally perceived or portrayed.

27. Your conscience is the signal that guides and reminds you of your moral compass and keeps you from engaging in acts that are wrong, harmful, or demoralizing. Override its warnings and you will grow to ignore its alarming judgment and later realize you are deeply rooted in a life of sin and foul habits. Be wise and heed your conscience while it is strong and effectual, for it is the insurer of a high quality and noble life.

28. Before every act or expedition you must ponder a realistic conclusion, determine all of the actual possibilities, and always inquire with extreme caution. However fraught with risk, assumption is key to discovery.

29. Teaching becomes futile when the substantiation of its concepts are inapplicable. The wise will always teach with relevance every course essential to wisdom, health, and prosperity.

30. To teach is to instill in the mind a compilation of information regarding the intricate features and purpose of specific concepts or entities. By acknowledging what you've learned and the sources through which you've been taught, you may come to identify your mental programming, conceptual

perception, intuitive judgment, and why you believe and pursue the things you do.

31. I must inform you that as you go on entertaining yourself and giving your time and efforts to many activities that comprehending the phenomenons of life is your primary objective. Remember, until you are capable of fathoming these phenomenons you will remain in wonder, awe, and ignorance.

32. If the presence of wisdom can be educed from all things how is it that so few are able to perceive it? The key to entering the sacred chambers of wisdom is to understand the realities before you and thoroughly analyze each of their features to discover every truth concealed within.

33. Since you are bound to the arrangement and conditions of your beliefs, faith, and intellectual resolution, you may devise and develop solely with the elements and aspects of those dimensions perceived and accessible to you. Commence to imagining and pursuing beyond your common ideals, realities, and activities.

34. Without the awareness of existing entities, anonymous sources, or obtrusive forces operating behind an occulted veil you may be subject to powers and sophisticated orders set in place to direct the course of your life. These realities may greatly affect how you may otherwise perceive your beliefs or administer your actions and the direction of your life.

35. Those who are weak, uninformed, or incompetent with a particular ability or activity must look to others whose strength and skills will compensate for their lack of power, knowledge, or capabilities. In any state, one must strive to learn and be of great subsistence and universally masterful, for the abilities gained through self-sufficiency are by far the greatest attributes of freedom and achievements one may ever acquire.

36. What can happen is much greater than what has happened. For what has happened is no more, but what can happen is only a few junctions away from occurring. Waste no moment, for each one is rapidly peeled away from your existence.

37. Everything one does incites the cause and effects of numerous eventualities. The objective is to acquire the knowledge and abilities required to activate, deactivate, or effectively utilize the function of every event to accord with your plan. Use whatever resources, information, and entities you have to increase your power and perfect your ability to facilitate advantageous activities.

38. Cause your mind to inquire and link from one source to another successively and you may gain access to and influence or control over sources and entities extensively beyond your central position.

39. Consider wisely what you pursue. Not all of your quests will transpire or end the way you may have imagined.

40. Doing for others is preparing the way for others to do for you. Live this way and you may realize all things are available to you. Many things you desire are hidden within and may be acquired through acts of compassion and generosity.

41. The wise acquire and conserve only what is essential for a productive life and conceive and express only those thoughts that attribute to the providence of their health, knowledge, and affluence of resources.

42. It is not the healthy who are in need of a doctor, but the ill. Therefore, go and learn what the righteous are to sinners.

43. There is no inverse to an act that has already occurred. However, it is wise to restore what can be mended and establish an effective prevention for what you do not want to occur.

44. Few are able to exact the order of events. With the perceptive in which you perceive a matrix, you may respond and counter the effects of every situation appropriately. Through correct judgment and a prudent application of thought, you may incite events to develop as you desire.

45. Those who are more competent or stronger than others should not exert their strength and abilities over them but should be rather modest and tactful.

46. The wise reveal their power only when they wish to make known their abilities and use them only when absolutely necessary.

47. It is true that a person or entity usually possess the very nature, essence, and qualities of their origin. However, things, people, or any other living being should not be characterized solely by the source from which they derive nor by the concepts of the system in which they are established, but rather by their own unique functions, characteristics, purpose, principles, and motives. Not all things are subject to the likeness of their creator, possessor, or identical aspects of their nature.

48. When faced with hardships or setbacks one must not dwindle into a state of stagnation and weakness. Instead, he or she must persist in self-discipline, confidence, and faith. One must search, find, and utilize the entities and sources that will provide the knowledge, motivation, and high-spirited attitude one will need to overcome all adversities and continue to live a passionate and active life.

49. The power of intention is activated by these three words; what you do. The most essential and powerful qualities of the mind are the ability to acquire and utilize information, and awareness. The wise are productive, constantly learning what is required to sustain a lucrative and viable future.

50. Those who demonstrate an exceptional level of sacrifice beyond their means and expectations for the sake of others are true loyalist. Such individuals deserve to be held in high esteem and given the utmost respect by those who are fortunate enough to be the beneficiaries of their kindness.

WISDOM EXPOSED

III

SECTION THREE

1. Contemplate these virtues: knowledge, wisdom, and understanding. Grasp their essence, and they shall serve as a reliable compass, leading you through the obstacles of life's journey and propelling you towards the attainment of your most cherished aspirations.

2. All that you do becomes intrinsically formal to your development and initiates the beginning or end of every situation you encounter.

3. Before one may assume responsibility or is acknowledged as independent, he or she must fully understand the importance of liability. Be wise and know that one has observed the conduct and behavior of others and is merely mimicking their actions or complying with what they've been influenced, forced, expected, or taught to do. When teaching, always practice and inculcate the importance of self-awareness and accountability.

4. The act of idling signifies a lack of purpose that can ultimately result in undesirable consequences. Instead, one

should strive to live a life filled with unrelenting passion, relentlessly pursuing the limitless facets and marvels of life.

5. Adamant faith, profound knowledge, and unshakable confidence will break through all obstacles. Neither spiritual nor physical barriers can hinder those who possess these virtues from accomplishing their goals.

6. The more you devote yourself and insist on a desired result while intelligently and sensibly dealing with those who oppose your advance, the closer you are to fulfilling your goal. When dealing with adversaries direct your faith and actions with extreme precision and you may achieve the victory for which you are earnestly striving.

7. Virtue and vice lie both in passivity as well as activity. One who leads a life of tranquility and reflection knows when to participate or refrain from participating in the affairs of the world.

8. Life circumstances can either create confusion and disorder or joy, order, and serenity within the soul. It is crucial to focus your attention and efforts on pursuits that will fill your essence with genuine happiness and enthusiasm. By doing so, you can maintain a youthful, purposeful, and prosperous spirit, ensuring your overall health and freedom from stress.

9. True freedom is understanding and having control over your circumstances, being where you truly desire to be, accomplishing your goals with satisfaction, living life the way you envision you should, and being joyfully content with the conditions of your entire essence. Anything outside of this is soul-searching and striving to achieve these goals.

10. The level of faith that others have in you is directly proportional to the faith and belief you have in yourself. Your competence and capability are determined by the effort, energy, and determination you put into your performance.

Understand that the intensity of your passion and confidence influences others to support you in achieving your goals. Therefore, it is crucial to exhibit unwavering determination and commitment to your objectives in order to inspire and motivate others to assist you with the process of your goals.

11. Those who succeed far beyond their goals realize deep concentration, a great deal of effort, self-motivation, courage, steadfast faith, bold risks, thorough preparation, and the ability to coordinate cooperation are the high-minded traits required to fulfill any objective worthy of notable achievement.

12. The absence of essential resources often impedes the growth and progress of those requiring moral, spiritual, educational, or financial support. Nevertheless, eliminating unhealthy habits, and counterproductive behaviors from those lacking knowledge, struggling with addiction, or lacking discipline can lead to recovery, growth, and a transformation into stronger, more knowledgeable, and intellectually astute individuals. The discerning recognize the appropriate actions to take, whether it be to give or withhold, in any given circumstance with justice and propriety.

13. Indeed what you encounter is real. However, you must acknowledge the fact that there are intellectual and supernatural influences involved with everything we experience. Many things are established, developed, and carried out secretly or with illusive conduct.

14. To develop a dexterous character and astute mind, one must master the master's most difficult teachings and become his or her most consubstantial pedagogue. This is the method prescribed for attaining wisdom, increasing strength, and ensuring the assurance of success and wholeness.

15. Followers will pursue and support those with a purpose beneficial to their needs or those willing to perform those deeds they are reluctant or unable to perform themselves. Be

wise to inquire and determine whether one's plans will achieve the results you desire and hope to have fulfilled.

16. For the common populace, sustenance and indulgence serve as the primary motivators of action. However, for the enlightened sovereign, the paramount focus is on fostering mass order and control through concise guidance and methodized development.

17. It is of great importance for every young person to have wise and productive mentors to instruct and advise them in the process of noble pursuits. The absence of virtuous role models can cause many to go astray, allow them to engage in damaging behaviors, adopt negative self-perceptions, and embrace unsavory ideals.

18. Those who develop resources and devise entities that produce provisions are by far more responsible, capable, knowledgeable, comfortable, and financially secure than those without them. Strive to be one with such power and affluence.

19. Surrounding you are an infinite array of entities, realities, and sources that are waiting to be utilized by you. You are an intelligent being with a creative force within you to commission all things. Use what you have within and what you have access to wisely and surely you will excel beyond your current position. However, those who do not realize their creative potential and gain control over their being and the circumstances affixed to them will find themselves living under the conditions, regulations, sources, energy, ideas, and authority of those who are better established, equipped, and much more resourceful. To be free from the binds of society's common conventions and those claiming dominance or supremacy, it is imperative to hone the skill of perceiving and accessing higher levels of abundance while steadily cultivating a more dominant and resilient essence.

20. Whatever you give immediate attention to becomes the center of your reality. With that you may prefigure the avenues you may choose to arrive at various destinations.

21. Obligations are to those who are seized by predicament and freedom to those who have learned to live free of all liabilities. The wise are responsible in all they do, living free and happily with exhilarating passion.

22. Never substitute your aspirations for something of lesser value. Instead work diligently until your greatest hopes are realized.

23. Miracles and exquisite realities are for those who believe in life, for they realize they exist in such an exquisite reality and that nothing is more miraculous than life itself.

24. This and everything surrounding you reveals the essence and forces of nature. All things adhere to what nature devises, compels, and permits them to be or do.

25. Indeed you lack knowledge, wisdom, and understanding. You are merely assessing matters according to your circumscribed intelligence.

26. The things that hold us in awe often lose their power of amazement and astonishing appeal as we grow used to them and claim to have a full understanding of their purpose and being. However, those who are appreciative will revere the essence of all creations perpetually even if they are fully enlightened to understand every detail of their being.

27. All things come to the conscious mind only after they have been exposed, acknowledged, and understood. Regardless of how conspicuous things may appear, all things are not immediately perceived or understood.

28. A place is but an entity used to carry out various forms of activities. Though they may be other than what the mind perceives them to be in all their many features, until such inferences are made, they are nothing more than abstract structures.

29. Acknowledge first all that you are capable of then determine with wisdom what you will do with those abilities. Seek counsel from those who are wise and noble in all their ways.

30. Self-discipline keeps one from being enthralled by profane concepts and fascinating objects. Remain self-controlled and content, this way you will acquire only what will increase the strength of your essence and the capacity of your knowledge and prosperity.

31. Those who are purposively observant to a particular subject or objective may acquire the concepts, knowledge, techniques, and skills necessary to thrive in that subject or objective. Continue to study and you may master the art and receive the wisdom proceeding your diligent efforts.

32. Even nature is willing to reveal many of its most intricate secrets. Do not think those you have cannot be unveiled and exposed.

33. In everything there is something undiscovered. There is always room to inquire, investigate, and experiment.

34. In every moment and every event there is an infinite multitude of realities present. The question is which of those realities you are aware of and attentive to during those moments and how you perceive and react to them.

35. For one to prove him or herself confident he or she must develop a spirit of courage which is required to overcome the test of fear and doubt. Build courage and your faith will lead

you through many adventurous exploits and into the bliss of many glorious victories.

36. Unity is akin to trust, and their greatest enemies are deceit, treason, and secrecy. When they meet there is an unpleasant dispute, and the damage will not be easily mended. It is much wiser to understand the importance and commitments of trust, for you will be obligated to uphold the requirements of every vow you assume.

37. Many things exist. However, what you do not have knowledge of remains veiled and could be of great significance to the function and order of your reality. Focus your mind and remain vigilantly attentive so you may become aware and informed of what is now beyond your perception and cognitive capacity.

38. The habits, routines, conduct, attitude, and characteristics of every person will be exposed to receive recognition. Even what one tries to keep secret will eventually be unveiled. Those who are honest and morally inclined usually have nothing to hide.

39. Joyful, confident, and positive energies invigorates, heals, strengthens, and fortifies the body and spirit with the essential vitalities of life. Pursue habitually the activities and sources providing these energies and you will live a strong, enduring, and purposeful life.

40. It is under the pressures of adversities that success is most sought and usually achieved. However, it comes only to those who refuse to abandon their goals and passion to acquire greater levels of prosperity.

41. Possessiveness, impulsiveness, heedlessness, and idling are the erring ills of humanity. The wise are inclined to devise effective methods to expunge and replace these destructive

traits with the high qualities of intense study, perseverance, and diligence.

42. To avoid foreseen danger or chaos you must go where you will find peace and safety.

43. Nothing is the same from one moment to the next and no matter how immutable things may appear there is always change.

44. No material object is yours to possess forever. Therefore, use what you have to advance upon your desired status than give them away. By doing this you will make space within your essence to attract new entities that will advance you even further.

45. Many things of old are more valuable than those that are new. Be wise and distinguish what will be of greater significance and an asset to your future.

46. Words like actions have the power of manifestation. Whether these words actualize the purpose and reality for which they are invoked depend entirely on the source from which they derive.

47. To ensure unsurpassable strength and certain victory you must perform vehemently to build a solid, powerful, and knowledgeable essence with a physical structure that is impenetrable. If your foundation and structure are not built to be infallible there is a chance you may be conquered by the force of others greater in strength and intelligence.

48. Discipline is the key to good health, prosperity, and a long and happy life. Those who are wise do not desire anything that does not attribute to this truth. However, many will endure the hardship that comes through ignorance and inadvertence.

49. To acquire a life of prosperity and high quality one must attain the wisdom to perceive arid and impoverished environments. By all means, gain knowledge and pursue success so you may remain free of immoral conduct, and unhealthy habits and improve discordant communities.

50. Individuals who possess the wisdom to consciously and intelligently refine their character will undoubtedly chart a path towards success and cultivate a heightened foresight of the challenges they may face. Your perception and actions in every situation holds the power to shape your character and determine the trajectory of your life, ultimately resulting in the realization of your unique reality, whatever that may entail. It is through conscious choices and deliberate actions that we mold ourselves into the person we aspire to be and pave the path towards our desired destination.

WISDOM EXPOSED

IV

SECTION FOUR

1. Few are the elite who embrace and study the teachings of wisdom. These few will prosper and inherit endowments far greater than those with great riches and bricks of gold could ever afford.

2. Worth and value are perceived differently by each person. What is of immense importance to one may be worthless to another.

3. A cohesive society cares and nurtures the physical, mental, and spiritual welfare of all its members, even extending its support to distant communities. In contrast, individuals dwelling in discontented or apathetic environments tend to disregard the development, needs, and aspirations of those beyond their immediate circle, exhibiting little or no interest in promoting their physical and intellectual advancement and well-being.

4. An angry person is not content with his or her circumstances and may express or release unpleasant emotions upon others. Consider how you may assist such a person to improve his or her situation and quality of life.

5. There is immense power in stillness and even when latent, in many things, there is a force being charged.

6. Love is by far the greatest force in life. However, it is not administered amongst the people enough to achieve its full and true potential and for this many have and continue to suffer.

7. It is not solely circumstances that bring about the results of a situation but how one responds to those circumstances. Competence and faith are inerrable, therefore, in every situation, the wise are able to devise advantageous opportunities.

8. If you enable individuals to be what they are this they shall remain. However, if you influence and persuade them in a manner that will encourage them to believe in what you desire for them to be, this they will learn and may become.

9. Once the portal of higher quality has opened you must enter. As you advance you must never turn back or succumb to anything that will cause you to fall into a state of degradation.

10. Upon the fulfillment of a desire or achievement you must immediately devise a new project or adventure to keep yourself from loafing. You should never lose your passion, motivation, or determination to increase your multitude of achievements.

11. Before one can be assigned to handle matters of great significance one must first prove that he or she is responsible with minor obligations.

12. As evolving beings every person is where they are in order to understand and learn from every experience that they can and must progress. Through the things we do everyone will

advance from one situation to the next in accord with the thoughts and actions they apply to every event. Those who do not strive to make noticeable progress will remain stagnant in their current condition until they consciously improve upon their thoughts and actions. Only then will one prevail over the events withstanding.

13. Sacrifices of the most valued things are essential for further development. If sacrifices are not made willingly and with full awareness of the purpose and benefit of those detachments, one may miss what is greater to his or her evolvement.

14. Hardship, suffering, defeat, and setbacks are the tests and trials given for resilience and improvement. Those who receive these tests yet continue to stand firm and prevail in the face of those challenging events will become more intelligent, durable, and adaptable beings.

15. Negative thoughts, foul deeds, and indecorous language deteriorate the nobility of one's character. Guard your mind and spirit so that no immoral person or vile concept will corrupt your dignified qualities and high standards. Continue to uphold and sustain a genuinely honorable and prestigious character.

16. Be still, for there are millions of events, activities, ideas, people, tangible objects, and mechanical devices competing for your attention. Focus solely on those things that are productive, advantageous, and contributing to the fruition of your highest aspiration. You must see the big picture while focusing on the integral factors that are essential for fulfilling your existential purpose.

17. Since you have the power to choose the methodological nature of your thoughts, you also have the responsibility of determining whether your thoughts will aspire to godly and positive intent or debasing and negative intent. It is wise to

harbor and emit only those thoughts that are wholesome and inspiring.

18. For those who are deeply involved with sinful acts it may be too late. However, those who are pure and noble in all their ways hold the keys to prosperity and blessings for future generations. It is our duty to protect them by example.

19. There are many things that are not to be indulged. Therefore, acknowledge the purpose and benefit of all things and determine whether those events, concepts, and entities are beneficial to your well-being.

20. Every situation has its own unique matrix, circumstance, and effects regardless of any presumption of regularity. If you are not an exact precision designer of such events, you must expect every event to develop with divergency.

21. All thoughts relating to intellect are interpretations of one's perception of particular observations or someone else's suggested perception of those observations. However, individuality lies in your ability to analyze and categorize the notion of every concept and create for yourself a very unique perception and idea of all things.

22. Speaking and every method of communicating are magnificent abilities attributed to humanity. It is wisdom to have your words filled with truth, inspiration, faith, and the power to actualize.

23. What a miracle is for one may be a simple feat for another. And what one imagines another may actualize.

24. Just as the blending of specific elements can alter the fundamental nature of a substance, the same principle applies to the realm of human intellect. It is imperative that every alliance strives to yield harmonious and favorable outcomes.

25. Every law is a concept, an idea devised by the thoughts of one person who then employs and convinces others to agree and enact the reality of those ideas with the hope of being protected or rewarded by them. However, those who are not aware or are in opposition to those impositions are subsequently subject to experience the consequences of those laws which are also devised by one and agreed upon by others who will be concordantly protected. Be wise and extremely cautious of those who are obtrusive and insolent.

26. Everything derives from an active source; some are perceivable, and others are too secreted to fathom. The fountain of life bestows its grace in many forms, and you are one.

27. Before existence there is nothing. Yet by the incomprehensible mysteries of inception, something brings forth the essence of all things and sustains all that exists. The truly enlightened acknowledge their divine presence.

28. Pursue and embrace the activities, events, and entities that will lead you to your desired destination. As you do, you will find that life can be very propitious and overflowing with opportunities.

29. The realities set up before you, comes through you. They reveal your very self and could not be without you.

30. Every able person begins life with equal physical faculties and cognitive capabilities. The difference in mannerisms, perception, and capabilities derives from the establishment, subsistence, and conventional standards of one's ancestral conduct and the way one perceives and responds to his or her ancestral ideologies and deeds.

31. When a person is haggard by numerous adversities a cloud of doubt abides in the minds of those who witness the affliction. However, if that person overcomes the affliction and

prevails in prosperity, every witness shall admire and adorn him or her with praise and honor.

32. Those who doubt must see to believe, but the faith-filled have confidence in what they believe. With both there is expectancy.

33. There exists a scientific framework, a cognitive equation, that incites all supernatural phenomena. With the proper interfusion of elements and purposeful incitement of definitive actions, one may create any event, essence, or entity he or she desires. For this reason, every action of the wise is thought out with preciseness and executed with precision.

34. There are always more comfortable circumstances and profound realities waiting to be explored and experienced. A life of luxury and serenity is always available; however, you must work with diligence to accomplish the objectives necessary to acquire and sustain such lofty stations in life.

35. Prosperity rewards its captors with harmony, gratification, excellent health, contentment, and plenty of excess. This fortune is attained solely through self-confidence, the pursuit of courageous endeavors, and many exceptional achievements.

36. Keep everything in your essence pure and holy and blessings will come upon you like warm days and flowers to spring.

37. If you ascribe perseverance and incessant deeds to a specific goal you will develop strong abilities and produce the evidence and product of your faith. Do not allow the lack of creativity or setbacks to stagnate or prevent you from going beyond to encounter amazing experiences and wonderful places. With creativity, there must be a firm commitment and organized efforts. Devoid of these, your ideas and aspirations will remain futile and unfulfilled.

38. Every person is a creative and active source of life, therefore, the wise acquire many associates and receive from each of them entities and sources that will fortify the affluency of their success.

39. Surely your culture is a system of ideologies and automatons to which you yourself are too attached and consumed to deviate its order and acquire a life of true freedom apart from its ramified assimilation. Do not become too attached and reliant upon society's economical superstructure or you may become so dependent upon its systematic function that you are enslaved by its order for many years to come.

40. There is information that is incorrect, obsolete, or irrelevant. To attain truth you must inquire of those who have it or if possible achieve it through your own efforts and experiences.

41. You should be always observant and intently alert so that you may have a clear prevision of what may transpire and avoid all physical harm or immoral conduct.

42. You devote yourself only to those things you earnestly accept and prove you believe through your actions. All other concepts or conducts opposing your beliefs are considered unacceptable at least until you are persuaded to believe differently.

43. It is wiser to approach the junction of a path knowing which way you will go rather than relying on chance to fate you. Those who know the direction they must go understand what is required to reach their desired destination. The wise become knowledgeable, perceive their destiny, and are prepared for what may be encountered along the way.

44. With every experience you will acquire knowledge and may also devise and direct situations as they occur. Make noble

decisions and realize you are responsible where you have a choice.

45. It is much worse to be immorally defiled than it is to be sternly disciplined. Understand, the pains endured through discipline will subside quickly, but a mind without high standards and strong morals will ruin the quality of many generations to come. Always administer discipline with the intention of instituting excellent qualities and high esteem.

46. True discipline teaches one to adhere to the correct course of conduct. However, merciless punishment creates resentment and distress.

47. The acceptance of discipline deserves mercy, and earnest penance deserves a modified punishment.

48. Not all things are for the eyes or the ears. However, both may perceive the essence and nature of many things.

49. Detach your mind from every entity and activity and you will sense and feel them pull at you and attempt to attract and possess you. Reject the influence of these material, sensual, and ideological ties and refuse to oblige their obligations and they will rage against you and watch you intently to see what you will do with your divine abilities. Prove that you are in control, completely content, and truly at peace within and they will submit to your authority and respond in accordance with your will. Read this again.

50. For the sound, attentive mind, knowledge, and prosperity are easily acquired. To attain true peace one must find a place that provides comfort and tranquility and enter the Realm of Meditation which is free of all worldly influence. When the mind and spirit are at peace and free of all anxiety one may devise and produce whatever he or she desires with great efficiency.

V

SECTION FIVE

1. Your body, mind, and spirit are in essence very much like a consecrated monastery and like this temple they must be kept clean, peaceful, and holy. Ponder and acquire this state of wholeness.

2. Those who are endowed with the wisdom of self-esteem abstain from undignified conduct out of respect for their character rather than the censures of common edicts.

3. Only those whose minds and thoughts are imbued with knowledge, wisdom, and understanding possess the ability to wield mastery over the agents and forces of life. It is through the acquisition and application of these indispensable qualities that one can assert authority and command over all operatives, ultimately establishing a functional and harmonious existence.

4. Keep your mind from engaging and giving attention to frivolous activities occurring around you and you will discover many exceptional and productive activities are available to you as well. Search for advantageous opportunities and train your mind to be equable and free of all mental and environmental stress.

5. Knowledge gained is the beginning of understanding and understanding the dawn of wisdom. However, without the qualities of virtue, one may never discover the doors that lead to true prosperity.

6. Your principles and beliefs will be revealed and validated by your conduct, and an adamant stance in those beliefs will provide substantial evidence to prove you are indubitably true to your ideals.

7. Whatever a person goes through they must learn and gain wisdom from their experiences. The wise are prudent, avoiding every detrimental situation or perilous environment, and advance intelligently through every event they encounter.

8. It is better to sit alone meditating or studying than it is to place yourself in the company of foolish, idle, and immoral individuals.

9. It is not always beneficial to go after the things that attract your attention. If you are not intently focused on productive goals many things may draw your attention to trivial activities and distract you from fulfilling more important tasks. Keep in mind the true path and pursue it with extreme urgency.

10. Be attentive and take nothing you care for granted or you may lose it.

11. A man who owns more than he can carry in two bags and strives for worldly desires more than he does for wisdom is considered a worldly man and even if he owns only two bags, if the contents within those bags are not intended for noble purposes, they will hinder him from ascending into heaven.

12. The state of autonomy and great sustenance derives from the awareness of social development, cultural ideals, and the understanding of one's presence within a specific environment. It

is through this process you will find a location suitable to establish, build, and fortify your desired estate. The extent of your power lies within your faith, knowledge, and abilities.

13. Whatever fills you with purpose and provides you with endless joy and a life of ease, this is what you must attribute most of your time, effort, and energy to. Focus on what you believe will produce for you the object of happiness and much success.

14. It is not in reaching the completion of your goal where you benefit most, but rather through the trials, experiences, and accomplishments encountered along the way. Always perform with preciseness so you may have a full recollection of every factor applied to the process of achieving your goal and be certain the efforts you apply will always achieve the results you desire. Above all recompense for your merits, learn to value your abilities, time, and efforts.

15. The magnitude of your faith, achievements, and competence will surely determine and reveal the potential of your ability to advance successfully through every trial or endeavor. Every goal you complete or obstacle you overcome will enhance your potential to develop a stronger essence and a more dominant demeanor.

16. The infinite storehouse of information is much too extensive for one to retain even a tiny fraction of all that is adduced. Continue to inquire and search for the true meaning, purpose, facts, and data of every significant matter.

17. To get somewhere, you must leave somewhere, and to acquire something you must part with something. Indeed, the more attentive you are to one thing the more you neglect the others.

18. You must examine your social status by the way you are acknowledged by others, your authority within a specific social

setting, and your ability to acquire what you desire. From time to time, you must evaluate the stance and condition of your essence and demeanor.

19. True wisdom is hidden from foolish and rebellious individuals, and the path leading to it is long and strenuous. It requires tremendous effort to find and persuade the teachers of wisdom to accept you as their student.

21. Those who are skilled in the arts of production shall accumulate wealth. However, all employees will assist in building great provisions for the owners of such enterprises and yield much less. The wise are inclined to develop productive entities and resourceful establishments.

22. Set your mind adamantly on those events and situations you desire to experience, and you will advance upon and eventually encounter them. Let your aspirations be evident through the exertion and fruition of your actions.

23. Those who are optimistic, determined, and willing to encounter and endure many trials, obstacles, and adversities will acquire the strength, authority, and power to advance and accomplish many endeavors. Such a person is industrious and remains unyielding.

24. Resilience and diligence may prevail over the disappointment of failure and unless the results are injurious there is no harm in failing. Therefore, until you've mastered the objective you may persist.

25. Examine your whereabouts, activities, habits, and conduct. For as you do, this you sow, and what you sow will surely bring forth the fruit of your actions. This proverb will shine like the sun upon all your deeds.

26. People are always more inclined to work voluntarily for a noble cause and for those in need than they would for monetary rewards.

27. Because one complies with certain concepts, standards or conditions does not mean that person fully understands the truth or agrees with the motives behind the purpose of those ideas. Those who enter an agreement without first acquiring an absolute understanding of what they will receive, give away, or permit others to have or do lacks prudent judgment and are ignorant of the power of persuasion and influence. But even worse are those who exploit and manipulate those who are ignorant, for they are recklessly eager to gain what is not theirs.

28. Always consider the nature and motive of one's objectives then assess the matter to accord with your desire. If one's intentions are honorable you may accommodate the issue, but if they are not, you must administer correction.

29. Do not coerce or hoax others into an agreement or their pledge will be void and the agreement breached.

30. Many eyes have the ability to see, yet not all possess the ability to perceive.

31. Many have the ability to hear, but not all are heedful.

32. To try is the inception of failure, while doing is the process of achieving.

33. Bravery will shield you from a thousand enemies and adamant faith will provide you with the courage, strength, and capabilities to prevail over every adversity or adversary. If you believe you may advance with faith and confidence.

34. True harmony is found where love, honor, trust, and fairness are assured. A wise government prospers when it cares

for the communal quality and providential prosperity of all its people.

35. The mind being the most powerful force in the universe when it acquires a definitive understanding of life, its existential purpose, and a state of true harmony with nature, can heal all ailments, influence a burdened spirit to be at peace, and sustain its vital life force and physical presence indefinitely.

36. Faith is powered by the consistency of steadfast endeavors, unwavering confidence, endured perseverance, courageous deeds, and earnest beliefs. Pursue and develop these qualities and your ability to extrude and administer faith will increase and become one of the most eminent forces of life and the universe.

37. Do not succumb to low standards or conditions subject to inferior quality. Instead, advance solely upon those situations that are lofty, will improve the quality of your essence and cause your level of esteem to rise. Those who understand and live by these ideals must humble themselves to assist and teach those subject to poor standards and low esteem.

38. The power of laughter or even a smile can heal the body, elevate the spirit to bliss, infuse a bright personality, and help to develop personal relationships with many people. This force achieves its true potential when the nature of one's spirit is virtuous, positive, compassionate, and joyful.

39. Adversities produce within the valiant faith, willpower, an eager spirit, and a vehement desire to prosper. However, the doubtful, feebleminded, and passionless cower in self-pity and are subdued by circumstances.

40. Never underestimate the power of faith, for by it a determined mind certainly has the confidence and abilities to achieve its objectives. However, one's desire to succeed and

one's intellectual and physical capacity to do so must accord. If they do not one's desire may not be fulfilled.

41. Help and assistance are compassionate acts of faith. When appreciated those acts will increase the value of hope, faith, and passion of those who receive them.

42. Be patient and self-controlled in every situation even when others are rude or hostile. By doing this you may put them in a state of humility and cause them to show you favor and respect.

43. The ladder of diligence is placed firmly upon the wall of success. It is up to you to determine how extended the ladder will be and how high the wall will ascend.

44. Remain temperate and adroit in unpleasant circumstances and dexterous with what you have. Never allow yourself to be stagnant without a plan to develop, prosper, and increase your opportunities to advance.

45. Oneness with nature allows us to enter into a deep relationship with all the elements and spirits of life. In true harmony, we may interact with all the animals and creatures of the world, and enjoy communing with the water, plants, trees, stones, sun, stars, moon, wind, and even those who have passed on. For all of these are the great emissaries of life and the living essence of heaven.

46. Without proper training one cannot meet those critical moments when life demands a challenge. Prepare yourself to be masterfully skilled in all areas or face the realities of dreadful predicaments.

47. Those who do not find joy, peace, and great fulfillment in their work and everyday obligations have never considered their true purpose and desire or have not taken the correct path leading to it. In either instance, they have allowed themselves

to accept and become willing participants in a system that employs them to be common operatives. It is extremely imperative that as you pursue prosperity and happiness you do not become stagnate or settled in positions that are intended to be used as steps leading to your greater purpose.

48. A student is not above the teacher, but everyone who is fully trained will inherit the wisdom taught by the teacher.

49. To conquer your fears you must increase your level of confidence and build up the courage and will to go forth in faith. After considering the circumstances and effects of your actions, if it is absolutely necessary you must approach, engage, challenge, and compete with the object of your fear. Pass this test and you will acquire the audacity and inner strength to face every adversity or adversary that comes your way. It is always a wonderful feeling to stand confident and victorious over your opposition.

50. To those who believe in God, since the presence of this phenomenon is in you, anything you can imagine you have the power to achieve. For the faith in which you believe in God shall be infused in all you do and endeavor to manifest.

VI

SECTION SIX

1. To attain significant wealth, one must engage in the business of serving the masses by providing valuable resources such as manufacturing and product production, real estate, sought-after services, or various forms of entertainment. Business is the passion of those who desire to achieve the exhilaration of financial affluency.

2. There may be moments when you put in your utmost efforts only to discover that you have just barely begun to scratch the surface of what you hope to accomplish. However, if your objective is worth the exertion, do not falter. Continuously strive to discover new methods and innovative strategies that can expedite the achievement of your goals with greater efficiency.

3. The divine masters' commissions nature to construct the elements, dynamics, and laws of all that is actual and establish what shall be without revelation. Until you can fathom, manipulate and facilitate the mysteries of nature's phenomenal laws you may not escape the plans and fate it will bring upon

you. In any event, for your evolvement, the divine beings are willing to give you the wisdom necessary to free yourself from the force of nature's restrictive and dominating power. However, as with all understanding, you must inquire and discover logical explanations of how these supernatural laws are incited, enforced, and may be dominated and regulated. Have faith for it is possible to fathom what is now inconceivable and understand all of the dynamic functions of nature's agents.

4. It is wise to prepare yourself with extensive knowledge of the path you will travel before embarking upon a journey. Always study and consider what trials and obstacles may be encountered along the way.

5. When you desire something of true importance, worthy of many deeds and a substantial amount of energy, it must be pursued vehemently. Never substitute your desires or they will be repressed to immediate gratification and replaced with something less valuable and incomparable to what you truly desire.

6. Since the decisions and actions of one person can affect the lives and future of others, every person should be wise, trustworthy, noble, truthful, and considerate in all they do. The judgment of one can improve or ruin the lives of many.

7. Diligence is always better than laziness and boredom comes from a lack of productive activities. There is always a thrilling adventure or interesting project to engage in. Pursue and embrace the many exciting and propitious activities that will increase your passion and desire for life.

8. When seized and held by a force or entity exceeding your intellectual and physical abilities you must do all that you can to inquire and learn its most integral components, strengths, weaknesses, and imperative sources of vitality, and if necessary gain control over it.

9. Those who are absolutely certain and striving with heroic effort towards their hopes will cause everything required to achieve their goals to respond with approval and nothing will refute them. However, those who are idle or uncertain of their aspirations and purpose will be rejected earnestly by what does not agree with their intentions and are subject to experience the agony of many unfulfilled desires. The wise understand what they must achieve and align their every thought and action unwaveringly and confidently with every objective.

10. What may take one person years to achieve may be accomplished in a single day by another, and what is impossible for one may be very possible for another.

11. The perspective of concepts allows what one person dislikes another to enjoy, and what one is not willing to do another to do purposefully with extreme diligence.

12. By exerting effort to develop patience, circumspection, genuine concern, and the passion to fulfill a meaningful objective, you may increase your influence and establish for yourself an honorable reputation.

13. Perception is the providence of thought and with it you will give meaning and purpose to the many aspects of reality and live in accord with the premise of those concepts as you view them.

14. To increase probability towards the fulfillment of your goals, focus your efforts on the objective, isolate your thoughts to intense study, and increase the consistency of your determination.

15. Aspire, increase in faith, and realize your creative potential upon the essence of all things.

16. A loafing mind digresses and falls deep into the unproductive activities of idleness. However, those who apply their thoughts to meaningful activities will continue to excel in the most enchanting realities and acquire tremendous success through the advancement of many occupations.

17. Master the factors of prosperity and you will advance with competence in all of your endeavors.

18. Through knowledge one gains enlightenment and from enlightenment one studies to further understand. With understanding one becomes prudent with the subject in practice, then being completely knowledgeable and proficient with the commission of the subject learned one may teach the wisdom attained to others.

19. While the mind is to perceive, conceive, retain, and recall, the body is to respond to the demands of the mind. Be cautious and responsible caring for both so that you may live and sustain spiritual strength and excellent health.

20. Suppress immediate gratification and acquire self-discipline. By doing this you will prevent the stress of mental or physical defects and exhibit the attributes of a strong mind, body, and spirit.

21. When striving for a great cause do not allow your mind to drift away from the task you must concentrate on or you may become so distracted that you replace the deeds required to succeed with fantasies, unproductive activities, and idleness.

22. Through self-confidence, the appropriate use of time, and the proper administering of thought one may achieve the essence of any station or status envisioned.

23. To those who are optimistic hindrance is never perceived as defeat, but rather a time to reflect, reform, and re-establish.

This is the mind of those who are passionate, enthusiastic, and resilient.

24. The attributes of strength are developed through strenuous efforts, endured pain, and a perpetual strive to grow stronger. To enhance and sustain an essence of endurance and vigor remain active and refuse to abandon your objective.

25. Avoid self-pity which leads only to ruin. Instead establish and instill in your mind the powerful concepts of self-confidence, self-motivation, elevated esteem, and the assurance of achievement. This will enhance your ability to overcome adversities and prevail into a life affluent with success.

26. Before constructing a foundation you should know the quality of the sources and elements you will use to create what it is you are planning to establish. The concepts, sources, and entities you choose will determine the strength and quality of the foundation and structure you want to build.

27. Your perception and comprehension of concepts may not be understood by others as you understand them. However, if you explain and demonstrate those concepts with perfect clarity to those you desire to understand, they may acquire a thorough comprehension of your ideas and may even embrace them.

28. Ultimately all things are working as a collective force of mechanisms with the primary objective of providing whatever is required for you to achieve first your sense of purpose, and secondly to assist you with the many advantages that will allow you to develop the abilities and power necessary for you to achieve your state of divinity.

29. Self-control and contentment are the qualities required to refrain from succumbing to unhealthy habits and low standards.

Those who do not possess these qualities may stumble upon many calamities and bring themselves to ruin.

30. To prevail in patience you must master whatever causes you to become frustrated or agitated. Amidst all chaos, you must embody peace and remain equable.

31. It is not wise to destroy the essence of vital sources to acquire money or the selfish motive of what many refer to as a greater good.

32. The masterful are prudent and meticulous with everything they give attention to, and their plans are carried out effectively with honorable and uncorrupted deeds.

33. Being proficient in many arts, knowing the strengths, weakness, and abilities of one's workers and students, assigning appropriate tasks, directing with perfect guidance, disciplining to institute correction, knowledge, faith, wisdom, and understanding, acknowledging the habits, moral quality, courage, and truth in each individual, having an effective and productive plan and being prudent in all matters; this is the mind and wisdom of the masters.

34. Keep your spirit from pursuing and embracing the trends of the world and all its entities will become trivial. Infuse your spirit with a desire to possess these things and they will seem so significant they will cause you to chase after them with laborious effort. Whatever you pursue should embody the essence of virtue, knowledge, love, joy, success, and productive activities.

35. Those who find true peace receives a great fortune. However, to sustain it one must free him or herself from the burdens of the world and detach every emotional strain.

36. To be truly content eliminate all of your wants and produce or obtain only those sources that will supply all of your needs.

37. Pleasure comes through the attainment of desires pursued or acquired freely. It is important that you remain attentive and active with all that is in your possession and accessible to you.

38. It is not wise to make a single entity the sole source of your provisions, especially those that are not your own, but rather one of the many additions to your facilities. One must realize that when the owner of an entity no longer requires your service you should have other reliable sources sustaining you.

39. On the path to success one must know exactly what one wishes to attain and with preciseness how the objective will be achieved. Inquire to understand every reality of the subject or object you believe is worth pursuing.

40. Power belongs to whoever is knowledgeable and competent with the mechanisms and functions of a specific subject or entity, and honor to those who apply their power worthily.

41. An arduous task may be accomplished when it is perceived and understood correctly and commissioned intelligently. The objective of every goal is to devise a methodological strategy that will achieve the end of an acquired aspiration.

42. Many are creatures of outside influence imitating the interest of the majority. Rare indeed are those who possess the ability to think independently of their own ideas and remain free of conformity.

43. When advancing upon greater levels of prosperity you must dispose of many concepts, habits, and material possessions. Many things of old are not acceptable with the new.

44. Teach the children to be clean, moral, respectable, appreciative, and honest and they will learn to be prudent in

their judgment. It is your responsibility to love and educate the children.

45. Those who achieve the full enlightenment of divinity are responsible, dependable, trustworthy, noble, and clean within and throughout their entire essence.

46. Be consistent in your efforts to remain productive and you will be highly esteemed and greatly rewarded with many stations, wonderful events, and palatable conditions.

47. A lively and determined spirit develops its body and mind into something much stronger and wiser. The most demanding qualities of this process are discipline and faith.

48. When you decide to do one thing over another you will lose or gain a variety of opportunities. You must embrace those opportunities that are most beneficial to your success and conducive to your well-being.

49. To inquire the counsel of wisdom is wisdom to beget. However, to pursue, contemplate and study intently to find the masters' and retain the subjects one desires to understand is true prudence. It is imperative that you inquire and acquire the knowledge and abilities necessary to adduce wisdom from all things encountered.

50. Do not allow adversities or adversaries to dismay you, but rather, maintain a positive attitude and prepare yourself to endure and conquer every unpleasant or demanding situation with unwavering zeal and impregnable faith. No matter the circumstance, it is essential to remain passionately enthusiastic and confidently esteemed, for these traits will serve as the foundation of your resilience and perseverance in times of challenge.

VII

SECTION SEVEN

1. Within the hills of worthless rubbish and discarded belongings are also precious gems and many things of value. So too the presence of wisdom in all things.

2. In truth, some who are considered simple possess more wisdom than those who perceive themselves to be wise, and some students hold a greater understanding than teachers who believe themselves to be more knowledgeable. It is important to acknowledge the limits of your knowledge and recognize that universal enlightenment is not easily attained. There will always be areas within any subject that require further study and exploration.

3. When a student is present and attentive but still manages to fail, the shortcoming of that student rest upon the instructor's inability to teach proficiently. It is the responsibility of every educator to grasp the full attention of their students by presenting each subject with great interest so the student does not experience the lesson as null and meaningless. The goal of educating is for all who are attentive to fully comprehend and learn all that the educator presents. To teach is the most

obligatory liability which requires the masterful skill of presentation.

4. It is more difficult to perceive all there is to know about what is already presumed understood than it is to embrace that which one is completely ignorant of. For what is already presumed to be known or understood has been scrutinized, characterized, and accepted as an ideal concept. However, what is unknown has undergone little if any scrutiny and merits wonder and ample attention due to the lack of information available on its numerous aspects. Endless discoveries and truths may be found in that which is presumed understood, therefore, the wise seek to unveil and encounter many new characteristics that emerge from both the known and the unknown. Whether complex or simple, if you look beyond your circumscribed perception, you may find more than those concepts implied to any reality.

5. Those who give the impression of having much from them much will be expected. However, those who appear to have little the little they give will be considered more than what is expected. In either instance, it is wise to be altruistic and generous.

6. Be cautious of those who take but are never giving. Such a person is inappreciative and may take your kind deeds for granted. However, you should not allow this to keep you from being kind and merciful.

7. Characteristics are formed and developed by one's perception of social ideologies and attitude concerning every experience. You are ever revealing your personality and beliefs through your actions, speech, emotional expressions, habits, and circumstances with every occurring event.

8. All things are significant. Whether you realize their importance or not is irrelevant with regard to their being.

9. Infliction and regret teaches the valuable lesson of delinquency and error. Learn from those unpleasant experiences and you may experience fewer disappointments and acquire the characteristics of discipline and prudence.

10. When a wrong is committed one may believe he or she has gotten away and will not experience consequence. However, it is the soul that suffers the affliction and attracts the many forms of karma.

11. You will know who your true friends are and who truly cares for you when adversities arise, or you are burdened with distress. These are the occasions designed to test the authenticity of one's true concern and fondness for you and yours for them.

12. It is you who accept, reject, create, or destroy the events and realities of your life as they occur. More often than not it is you who incite, form, and allow your conditions to be as they are. It is you who must acquire the knowledge, passion, and ingenuity to order the status of your life, and it is your responsibility to establish, develop, prosper, and excel beyond the many objectionable realities you encounter.

13. Your life is similar to the configuration of a book. Each hour's a sentence, every day a paragraph, every week a page, every month a chapter, and every year a sequel. It is you who creates your character's demeanor, aspirations, and circumstances, gives acknowledgment to other characters, plans the storyline, and determines what the title will be. Be wise and pursue a life you believe is worth living as though you were composing and will publish a book worth reading.

14. Experiences are the events that fabricate and develop the traits of your character. Be mindful of every experience you encounter and realize all of them will be forever the property of your soul.

15. The mind contains trillions of conceptual realities it may use to devise an infinite array of ideas, entities, and events. However, you must not allow any of these realities to distract or prevent you from acquiring or manifesting those essential realities necessary to create and sustain a productive, exquisite, and exhilarating life.

16. Every entity has components, divisions, or operative workers with different purposes, functions, or authorities. Gain knowledge and understanding of these faculties and their functions and you may effectively utilize, commission, assemble, disintegrate, or implement these entities to accord with your objective.

17. Upon attaining full enlightenment of yourself, complete awareness of your environment, an accurate perception of the world for what it truly is, all it contains, and the numerous principles and concepts of its many cultural ideologies, you will have to make a conscious decision. You will either be one of its many cooperatives or you will be committed to your own autonomous and unique purpose. Understand, once the world has gained power over your mind you will crave its events, entities, and concepts, submit to its controlling forces, and become wholly subjected to its bureaucratic realities. Like a slave to a master or a child to a language, you will embrace it, become one with it, and be exactly what all of its other faculties are; a submissive operative programmed to embrace and sustain its pre-established order. Choose instead to live free by being and remaining universally vigilant in a state of true sovereignty. Indeed knowledge of many subjects and many sacrifices are required to attain this profound state of freedom and eminent power.

18. Like an incandescent lamp illuminating upon the darkest depths of the universe, so is your capacity of information when set upon the extensive data of all subjects.

19. Upon acquiring power and authority you must also acknowledge your responsibilities and boundaries. By the extent of your capabilities, you should determine what is by deed possible or extremely difficult to accomplish.

20. You learn to embrace and choose to believe those concepts and ideals impressed upon you. Acknowledging the reality of every concept you must ponder, inquire, conclude, innovate, devise, and recreate your own ideas and beliefs.

21. Quality and value are a matter of opinion. What is insignificant in worth or tainted condition to one may be of great worth and in excellent condition to another.

22. The way to enhancement and betterment is to harmonize yourself with greater spiritual and physical essences. This requires your letting go of low-grade concepts, doing away with foul habits, and taking up those that are of better, stronger, wiser, and healthier standards. To develop a healthy, confident esteem you must embrace the significance of spiritual enlightenment.

23. To be a king or queen one does not require a crown, throne, or kingdom. What is required, however, are high standards, selflessness, excellent morals, godly wisdom, prudent judgment, and noble characteristics. Such characters are befitting.

24. By assembling the appropriate ideas, spirits, forces, and elements of life to perform in accord with your objective, you will acquire the power and ability to enter or exit any event, situation, status, or realm with acceptance and harmony. Such alliances require the influence and wit of a dexterous and prestigious mind.

25. The power of suggestion may incite what one believes or hope for, and these may, as a result, empower one's creative

imagination to action. The key to actualization is hidden in and utilized through a zealous and faith-filled spirit.

26. Attract, accumulate, and amass all the information and tangible objects you may. However, without creative ingenuity, productive efforts, and an accurate application of these objects and information, all the concepts and material possessions you've acquired will be useless to your advancement and the fulfillment of your desires. You must seek to obtain solely those sources and entities that will perpetually enhance your intellectual aptness and physical abilities and bring you into a state of self-actualization.

27. Every wise soul is self-disciplined, serene, knowledgeable, strong-willed, content, and aspiring with earnestness to achieve the supreme objective. Believe so that you too may acquire the phenomenal essence of divinity.

28. How and what are the questions of supreme relevance when contemplating the inception of existence. Without truthful answers to these questions, all things will appear vain and in a state of nothingness. To understand the presence and purpose of life you must seek first the spirit and grandeur of mind.

29. The mind like the universe is profoundly replete and purposefully active, yet so extremely void and idle.

30. To incite a movement find a persuasive motive around which others may be influenced to rally your cause in a highly spirited manner and perfect harmony. Achieve this and you will create a force powerful enough to alter and infer the course of social standards and ideologies.

31. Regardless of how intimately related situations may be, every event designs a unique series of events. It is wise of you to be meticulous with many details of the activities occurring within and outside of your central environment.

32. There is a balance that must be maintained between society's intellectual influence and control over the masses through the programming of vigilant government agencies and the freedom to live a natural and unregulated life. Understanding and embracing this truth will liberate you from the binding legalities impressed upon the masses and place you with those free, autonomous, and sovereign beings.

33. Those who have faith are confident and motivated by their passion to succeed. They do not wait for others to help them but rather help themselves to the many opportunities and resources that are available and will assist in the fruition of their goals.

34. In the phenomenal provenance of life there is supreme wisdom and the miraculous vitality of omnipotence. You too have been given a small portion of this supernatural source of power and intelligence and with an accurate application, you too may devise a phenomenal essence just as divine.

35. Success belongs to those who can perceive and resolve their most consequential issues effectively, prevail over strenuous obstacles relying on sheer determination, are passionately resilient, and remain unfaltering in their pursuit to achieve their greatest hopes and aspirations.

36. Fear debilitates hope, shuns the confidence of those who waver and succumb to its illusionary effects, and forces many to abandon their goals. It is better to embrace wholly the power of bravery and remain fearless so you may sustain the infused passion of victory. This is the command of faith that demolishes the terrorizing presence of fear and enables you to advance boldly in the face of every dreadful reality. However, those who are vulnerable or timid must seek refuge and protection from the dangerous and great adventures of life.

37. Behind every witless act there exists a cogent motive. The wise will always focus vastly on the remedies required to increase the knowledge and wisdom of those subject to poor judgment.

38. Failure and shame may at times be greater inflictions in and of themselves as opposed to punishment. For the grief acquired through an undesired experience may be more distressing than any punishment may otherwise address.

39. Extremely fortunate are those who have never suffered the adversities of poverty, for it is one of the most demanding circumstances one may ever experience. However, those who do suffer the great burden of poverty must strive relentlessly and diligently to break free from its deprival grip as speedily as possible, for it suppresses the faith, motivation, confidence, hope, and desire for the prosperity of all who attempt but fail to acquire the knowledge and resources required to escape its languishing realities.

40. Consume and digest or dispose of what you have and you may clear your essence for whatever you desire to fill it with. What you have may be preventing you from acquiring what you wish to receive.

41. In the process of hardship or the event of a physical affliction one must acknowledge his or her deficiency or weakness and administer the proper remedies and actions necessary to regain strength. With faith and the consistency of healthy and productive activities, one may improve and prevail over every defect or affliction.

42. Like a rock set in the rapid currents of a river enduring its constant boisterous events, so every event that comes to you shall pass.

43. Every event or situation causes the mind to reform the personality and although one's character is frequently modified

the transformation usually develops over time and is rarely immediately or ever noticeable.

44. Like the large stones of the Rocky Mountains, you will remain complacent in the normality of daily events as you encounter them unless you are somehow forced from the position of your common state by the effects of your actions, the intentional or accidental acts of another being or by the natural force of nature. In either instance, the events consistent with the course of your normal stance and conventional activities will be radically altered.

45. Some situations and entities are more difficult to dissolve or escape from than others. In such events, you must endure and plan so that when opportunities are presented you will be competent and wise enough to advance successfully.

46. Those who organize or participate in an event should inquire to understand what may occur and attain the knowledge, abilities, strategies, and equipment necessary to control every situation that may arise during that event. Those who understand this have acquired the skills of preparation and organization.

47. It is not wise for one to reap from where he or she has not sown without the permission of those who have developed what they have been allotted. Instead, one should learn to acquire and establish what he or she desires using what he or she has without intruding on others belongings.

48. The behavior, speech, and habits of one's character and the circumstances and conditions of one's station and environment contain sufficient evidence to reveal the true nature and quality of one's current status and stature in life.

49. Dwell not on those things that were lost but rather on what you now possess. Recoup and re-establish. Be wise and know

to what you may apply this rule and the situation to which it does not apply.

50. Gain a deep understanding of the world around you, then utilize your creativity and ingenuity to bring forth the reality you wish to see. Life has the potential to exceed your expectations, provided you approach it with a combination of conviction and methodical planning. There are no inherent limitations that can prevent you from surpassing the boundaries that society imposes.

VIII

SECTION EIGHT

1. It is prudent to secure your financial stability, establish a firm foundation, and accumulate many assets before taking on the responsibility of a spouse and children. Doing so will alleviate many stressors and minimize the burdens on your family members.

2. The wise do not exhaust their resources, finances, and energies on what does not increase the advancement of prosperity. Instead, they conserve and acquire greater provisions and valuable assets that will enhance the livelihood and educational quality of society.

3. If leaders or government officials are living in healthier and more prosperous communities than any of the hopeful inhabitants of their nation this proves they are self-indulgent and have no understanding of the meaning of unity. Genuine leaders and honorable government officials understand the importance of unity and the welfare of their nation. They do not seek self-indulgence or live in prosperity while their citizens struggle. Instead, they actively engage in the lowest levels of society to build and develop it until it thrives to a point where they would proudly raise their own children. True

leaders share the same hardships as their followers and work tirelessly to overcome every challenge together. He or she is always willing to sacrifice greatly and will focus vastly on harmony and the complete success of his or her followers.

4. A dysfunctional government burdens its people with stressful obligations and undesirable circumstances. However, a prudent and well-organized government leads all of its people in peace, excellent health, and increasing prosperity. Every person must be considered indispensable and a valuable citizen within the order of their society.

5. The most effective laws are those in which everyone agrees and complies. Those who oppose or act out against these laws have not acquired a full comprehension for the purpose of these establishments or may feel excluded and discriminated against by those who devised and enforced those laws.

6. A homeless or poverty-stricken person is overlooked by many, but the rich draw much attention. The wise will always have compassion and receive the homeless with joy, giving them the befitting gift of hospitality. The rich shall humble themselves and embrace this glorious duty as a godly liability.

7. Generosity, kindness, mercy, and compassion creates a wonderful sensation within the soul, softens the heart, induce a joyful smile, and demonstrates the expression of love. What you give shall return to you in the form of something greater.

8. Every event is circumstantial and every circumstance the result of very explicit actions. Perceive the prelusive actions that caused these circumstances and you will acquire the wisdom to understand, regulate, avoid, change, or order future events.

9. Strive to undertake challenging tasks instead of opting for easy ones. By doing so, you will enhance your knowledge and hone your skills, making you an expert in your field. Additionally,

repetition is key. Regularly practicing and refining your abilities will result in significant progress and mastery.

10. One must be keenly aware of the consequences that their actions may bring forth. By recognizing this, one can evaluate whether the end result of their actions justifies the potential rewards or consequences. It's important to understand that every action, or lack thereof, can significantly affect the outcomes of all future events.

11. Your deeds are measured on a scale of morality and your actions reveal an accurate indication of what you are. Every person is evaluated by their mannerism, actions, and deeds.

12. Idealistically you are what you say you are and until proven otherwise, what others say you are. Give great consideration to the exhibition of your conduct and the image and character you desire to display.

13. Those who are able to maintain their upright and disciplined demeanor amidst a crowd of immoral or unruly individuals are to be admired and recognized as individuals with great wisdom and empathetic authority.

14. It is better to acquire knowledge and wisdom than to receive monetary gifts and material possessions. For money and material possessions without wisdom are subject to waste.

15. Wealth comes to those who pursue prosperity and poverty to those who tolerate deficiency. Both will encounter opportunities and both are subject to succeed or fail.

16. A reputable education is acquired solely through those who are properly educated. Many are sent to teach, but few are adequately prepared to do so.

17. To establish a solid foundation, it is imperative to ensure that all the necessary resources are at hand for construction

and to continue acquiring additional ones as needed during the developmental process. Success stems from a resolute will and is realized through knowledge and unyielding determination.

18. Letting go of things you are in possession of can be a difficult thing to do especially if you feel they are supportive entities. True strength comes when you've gained the knowledge and abilities to adapt, prevail, and discover you may live and succeed just as well without them.

19. At times it is wiser to advance unprepared than it is not to advance at all. The risk may be greater, however, knowledge, confidence and the potential for success may be your reward.

20. Physical objects may be rearranged and contorted, but the order of all things comes together through the mind.

21. Reality is the only matter of fact that supersedes concepts. All things will be as nature creates, designs, and allows them to be. Learn to diversify your perception.

22. Thought and influence are humanity's most powerful abilities. Those who use them wisely will devise conventional standards and ideas others will live by and may accomplish whatever he or she desires.

23. Competence and audacity bestow authority upon those who have them, and enlightenment ascribes understanding to those who wish to enter the realms of advancement.

24. Assumption is second to the imprudence of ignorance. It is wise to apply the efforts necessary to inquire and unveil the facts and truth of every matter before embracing what is assumed or presented.

25. The wise seek to learn, develop, prosper, increase the quality of humanity, and live joyfully. Do what you must to become an elite member of this highly esteemed clique.

26. Faith, knowledge, competence, and wisdom create the essence of power and prosperity. Perform courageously and you may activate and embody these powerful forces.

27. From beginning to end intelligent thought and actions are the fundamental implications of achievement. Devise the actual plans of your ideas and you may determine and enhance the status of your position with every decision and goal you complete.

28. Despite all the universe consists of and all that goes on in the world, life acquires and actualizes its existence through you. Reasoning you must acknowledge and justify your purpose.

29. Not every goal or desire is easily fulfilled. However, if you are willing to persist with steadfast concentration, determination, and meaningful efforts you may achieve the success you are pursuing. This vigorous charge of ambition will increase, energize and strengthen your faith and infuse your confidence.

30. The wise have learned the importance of discipline and avoiding idleness. However, those who refuse to embrace the significance of responsibility and maturity are subject to experience the ordeal of infliction and hardship.

31. The attributes, sustenance, and hidden dynamics empowering all realities as well as the creative secrets of nature are not revealed plainly without proper inquiry. Be informed and know that nature is willing to expose all things when they are rightly discovered.

32. Given that the concept of God represents the ultimate manifestation of all creation, it is prudent to strive towards attaining a state of divinity.

33. Because one has mastered a skill or acquired a position does not make him or her wise. A person is wise when he or she is

responsible and prudent with every decision and deals with every situation in the noblest manner.

34. By clearing your mind and cultivating a sense of equanimity, you may come to realize that all things are mere concepts that are inferred and implied by the mind. In accepting these concepts as reality, you comply with a version of truth that is subject to interpretation and fluctuation. You now have the power to revise and determine the purpose of all things. Think and manifest, for you are a creator.

35. The most complex conundrums are as basic arithmetic to the wise, for these are the very mysteries and premises on which they meditate and use to procure wisdom.

36. There are concepts and subjects that are beyond your ability to comprehend and far too complex for those who are unapprised to understand. However, with steadfast devotion an attentive mind may learn and achieve anything.

37. Looking is merely observing and any knowledge acquired from it attributes to very few aspects and factors of all that is actually entailed. It is better to inquire with a desire to understand all that is entailed by becoming as intimately involved as possible. To attain a full understanding of any subject direct interaction brings forth experience and comprehension in greater detail than what may be acquired as an outside observer. However, you must be wise and cautious with anything you choose to inquire about and are unfamiliar with.

38. At times the very thing you fear, do not understand, or refuse to engage in is exactly what you must embrace. Such encounters are necessary to enhance your abilities, knowledge, faith, and competence. Only those who are fearless, confident, and inquisitive will involve themselves relentlessly to understand and become familiar with the unknown.

39. Know your purpose and you may meticulously devise your future prospects. Realize, you are already actively fulfilling many objectives.

40. Nothing may exist without depending on allotted elements and dynamic forces to sustain their essence, vitality, longevity, and functioning structure. The wise understand this and work diligently to preserve and maintain propitious conditions and healthy faculties for every essence contributing to the vitalities of their lives.

41. Like the skeleton of a living vertebrate all things are covered with unique layers of some kind to serve as a form of protection. Remove this protective covering and you may discover, when meticulous, a vital stimulus, essential components, or emptiness. This method may also be applied to determine one's motives.

42. Patience is a journey of enduring and prevailing the events of time. The ability to remain physically active and mentally sound is essential for a long life, a poised mind and a well-conditioned body. Be patient with eternity in mind and you will encounter many events and partake in many activities within your lifetime.

43. When you open the door of intimacy you expose much more of yourself and allow the other person to reveal more of him or herself than what is expressed before the intimate engagement. The bonding of intimacy is much more intricate than the simplicity of a platonic friendship. Acknowledge the fact that an intimate relationship usually requires a commitment, emotional energy, a greater level of trust, and more often than not obligations. Put plainly, intimacy involves a great deal of responsibility.

44. There are times you will have to observe and analyze the concepts and perspectives of others from a spectator's position to understand the methodological ideas of their social and

procedural operation. You must inquire with caution so that you may fully perceive and comprehend their concepts and objectives before you participate in or embrace their ideals and activities. Not all functions are productive or beneficial to the condition and betterment of your life.

45. Acceptance and compliance with suggestive ideas, habitual norms, cultural beliefs, and common characteristics develop and form the ethical conduct and personality traits of every society. Every person and community is developed by their ancestral course of action and change occurs within the essence, quality, and stance of any community whenever one of its members or an outsider interferes and alters the quality of their standards and conduct or induce them to embrace foreign ideas and entities. In either event, they will either develop into a more efficient and nobler people or descend into a state of degradation and lose their sense of esteemed prestige. Be extremely cautious with every person that enters and influences your community and shun anyone attempting to defile or degrade the quality, essence, and high standards of your society.

46. Your reputation is handled by others, but your character is developed and protruded by you. Being aware of your presence and conduct you should always exhibit your character as one that is mature, intellectual, noble, creative, astute, faith-filled, and diligent.

47. Leaders rise and preside over those who are unable to acquire the skills and wisdom to organize and conduct their efforts and resources advantageously. However, those who are heedful will learn quickly to establish, produce, develop, and exert their skills and assets profitably.

48. Give considerable thought to where you are and focus profoundly on doing what will assure your development into what you aspire to be and acquire. Do today what will manifest the experiences you desire to encounter throughout your life

and lead you constantly to where you desire to be as the future unfolds.

49. The wise perceive every moment as a newly begotten event that is often foreseeable and realize every event is subject to contrast the consistency of normality.

50. One must exercise great caution in setting expectations, particularly regarding matters of time and events, as they are highly sensitive to predictions. The course of nature and its activities may not always convey as you expect, and a prediction is like a rainbow in the sky, you see it and just as quickly as you run off to show someone else, when you look back it's as though the event had never occurred.

WISDOM EXPOSED

IX

SECTION NINE

1. In life, there exist numerous paths, roads, and doors that lead to different destinations. Therefore, it is certain that a path leading to success is open and available to you, always waiting to be explored.

2. Even those things done in secret are subconsciously exposed. It is better to live a life of purity keeping your conscience free of all shame or guilt. This is the noble path of spiritual peace and dignity.

3. Trust is the most sacred of all gestures and as vital as the heart. Place it in the wrong hands and regret and disappointment are certain. You must be extremely cautious with whom you entrust this great benefaction.

4. Friendship belongs solely to those you can trust with the security of your life, family, and property. Only through many

trials and devotions does one acquire the privilege to retain the faithful title of friendship. Before this, all are merely associates.

5. A person willing to put a price over their moral quality or is willing to degrade or defile him or herself or anyone for any reason has little if any self-esteem at all. Such a person has lower moral qualities than those who know nothing of dignity and will be perceived as obscene, dishonorable, and a disgrace in the eyes of many. Such a person may also be forgiven, made whole, and come to achieve nobility.

6. Those whose thoughts are optimistic, pure, and noble will be endowed with joy, prosperity, and many friends. However, those whose thoughts are callous, coarse, imprudent, idle, or of evil intent are pursued by anguish, torment, and many enemies.

7. Many say they will but when the time comes to fulfill the objective you will learn their promise is as lifeless and hollow as the shell of a peach core without the seed and there will be no fruition. Rely solely on those who are honest and true to their word.

8. It is not wise to entrust your well-being to the care of those who consciously degrade or defile their own lives with hazardous and foul habits. If one is not greatly concerned about the well-being of his or her own life, how much more will that person earnestly care for the lives of others.

9. Loyalty is shown to those who in some way inspire either through commitment, a reverential performance, instilled intimidation, or acts of love and kindness and comes from those who believe such a person is worthy of this honor. To determine whether one's loyalty is derived through fear of adoration, and to appraise the true commitment of one's loyalty you must observe what that person is willing to sacrifice and the terms, limits, and conditions one has attached to their devotion with and without the test and trials you may imply as

well as those implied by the persuasive influence of others. Through this method, you may determine the true value and commitment of one's devotion. Know that there is no reward but faithfulness that can compensate for the honorable deeds of loyalty.

10. There are times you must sacrifice, persevere, and endure trials of suffering at great lengths to achieve the status, essence, and quality of what you truly desire. Many great rewards will be the result for those who perform vehemently to overcome and prevail over hardships. Be patient and endure those things you aspire to attain.

11. Loyalty and devotion are sustained by the consistency of truth and an unremitting commitment. Those who honor their commitment are adorned with high esteem, love, and integrity. However, those who are not truthful and trustworthy will lose the confidence, respect, and devotion of many.

12. No matter how unfaithful a person has been to you, if you remain faithful to your moral standards and ideals you will be regarded as one with honor and dignity. Patience and forgiveness are the way.

13. The universe may allow anything to occur, but it allows nothing to go in vain.

14. One must never express joy in the suffering of another no matter how deserving the punishment may be. Those who do are weighed down by hatred and torment within their soul.

15. Understanding that all things are transient, what the wise are most inclined to acquire are knowledge, wisdom, love, many companions, harmony, and their state of divinity.

16. You should always have a secluded place where you can relax in total serenity and comfort. A place of beauty, healing, and security where you can resolve and unwind in peace.

17. Beyond the presence of chaos, adventure, drama, and excitement are the realms of peace, silence, and comfort. Journey to those realms and you will find yourself settled in the wonderful essence of serenity.

18. You will dwell on anticipated or past events until you can understand them, lose interest in them, or come to a resolution. Be wise and know whether those events and ideas are worth the time, attention, and physical or emotional energy you will apply to sustain them.

19. No matter how strenuously you may try to pierce a glimpse into the future you may never do more than reflect on your anticipated speculation. You may inquire solely upon your own or another's past experience, stimulated imagination, or assumption.

20. Regardless of how much one has pondered and examined the factors of a subject or situation there is a chance those conclusions are inaccurate. Consider this, only an experienced and competent expert may be thoroughly accurate where his or her knowledge excels in the information attributed to the subject in question.

21. In many situations there will be trials or disappointments both anticipated and unexpected. Do not become distressed or impatient with either for the good as well as the bad situation provides opportunities. The wise appreciate and learn from every experience.

22. Those who doubt lose heart, their confidence fades and their power departs. Instead of doubting be strong, firm, and waver to no bad report and you will strengthen your faith to soar higher and bolder trusting that your hopes may be fulfilled.

23. Not all battles are won by the just and sensible participants and winning does not always grant the right to be entitled the victor.

24. What you pursue adamantly with passion and faith may be attained. However, what you do with what you attain is much more important than all of the efforts you've applied to attain it.

25. As soil, water, and sunlight nurture a seed, develop it into a root, then sprout it into a tree, thus all things attract to their natural elements and receive all that harmonize with the characteristics of their essence. In this same way, you will attract and acquire all that appeals to the features of your thoughts, philosophies, beliefs, and faith. Put simply, you will receive all that your character measures and merits. Be extremely cautious of where you are or may go and realize what is required for you to develop a strong and healthy essence, character, and life.

26. If only the eyes could see what one's heart truly desires. Have patience, for time will expose and allow you to analyze one's true motives, passions, behaviors, nature, actions, and qualities. Thus, the true desire of one's heart may be seen.

27. Those who find themselves placed under the authority of others or allow themselves to work for others must be shrewd, relying intently on their conscience and intuition to perceive with clarity what is acceptable and what they must not yield to. One may submit wholly solely to those who are tested and found to be noble, trustworthy, and wise, and whose intentions and objectives are aimed toward nobility, betterment, and progression.

28. Do not allow your mind to be consumed by concepts or material objects or you will find that you too are subject to obsolesce.

29. Place no material object ahead of your life or the life of others. For it has many, but you are one.

30. To risk your life for another is an honorable deed, but to do so for righteousness and the betterment of humanity will bring honor to your name for many years to come.

31. Demands are used by those striving to establish or maintain authority. However, requests are used by those who have a humbled alliance.

32. When you observe an offensive person or sense that someone has or is offending you do not try to defend yourself using the same negative manner in which that person has in his or her attempt to offend you. Instead, remain patient and rational so you do not disturb your harmony or mar your reputation and if possible gain control of the situation.

33. Through discipline you will maintain and control your possessions and avoid being enthralled by worldly objects and vile concepts. Contain and possess without being contained and possessed.

34. Your personality is an assortment of ideas. Therefore, bind to your character those thoughts and manners that will emit the impression you desire to display and live out.

35. Your thoughts are as active and more powerful than any chemical substance. Consider this, the wrong mixture will cause havoc, but a good formula will create blessings and success.

36. Beware of those who think irrationally and speak absurdly. If you are not wise and allow them to entertain you, you will fall victim to their foolishness and become what they are.

37. Arguing proves that one is distressed and not in control of the situation. Brace yourself so you will not be seen as one who cannot contain him or herself and lack good judgment.

38. Every mature and liable person must have the right to choose whether he or she will pledge allegiance to a government by acknowledging and consenting to its contract. This is how true citizenship should be established.

39. A well-established and proficient government works diligently to maintain prosperity for all of its citizens and establish all of them in happiness with many assets. However, an improvident and callous government subjects its citizens to scorn, debt, and recession.

40. It is better to be a creditor, therefore, increase and refrain from debt. Resolve to be no one's debtor. No sacrifice is too great to avoid the inferiority of debt.

41. Strive to perfect the essence and quality of humanity. Before seeking other worlds ensure that yours is in a state of divine order and true harmony.

42. Knowledge is advantageous, but prudence, diligence, and virtue conjure the masters. To become truly enlightened study medicine, science, and divinity.

43. Enticement and substance are the mind's greatest distractions. However, absolute discipline suppresses the crave for materialism and allurement.

44. Positive influence and moral examples are required for just governing. Without them, the people will oppose the law and demand proper justice.

45. Pride is linked with the appearance of success, but the wise have learned to replace it with humbled gratefulness.

46. No man nor woman is superior to the next, only smarter. Yet better are those who are tactful.

47. If only the oppressed would come together they could assemble a force strong enough to persuade or overpower their oppressors and gain equality. Stand up and rebel without fear in unity and you will receive justice.

48. In a corrupt government the rich may buy their way from the penalties of the law while the poor are punished severely without mercy. A just government will always administer equality appropriately regardless of one's social status and financial capacity.

49. Neither money nor gifts should be accepted as a means to escape justice nor should an officer of justice lie or disregard the law to benefit a personal motive or show favoritism.

50. Justice is in the mind of the righteous, but harsh punishment is sought and administered by the merciless. Be just and judge with a balanced scale of discipline and mercy.

X

SECTION TEN

1. It is wiser to gather yourself and leave everything to settle than it is to live a life overwhelmed by stress and worries. You should always reside within the essence of comfort, love, joy, beauty, and peace.

2. Motivational encouragement and influential support create prosperity and a desire to take up a noble cause. However, a rude and aggressive approach may cause resentment, fear, and rebellion.

3. Before the effects of true healing can occur one must acknowledge his or her spiritual, emotional, and physical state and determine the cause of every defect. One must then surrender whatever is causing or may cause further ailment and implement the appropriate remedies that will quickly restore one's health. Plan and perform to live a vigorous, robust, and active life by producing positive energies, creating blissful moments, and engaging in exciting activities.

4. Health is to uniformity and disease to asymmetry. Both are supremely the results of consumption and habit.

5. Apply your efforts to those activities that will stimulate and strengthen your mind, body, and spirit, and refrain from engaging in what will be hazardous to your health or shorten the duration of your life.

6. You should not always seek to rely on family and friends to pull you from adversities, for they are hoping you will overcome and prevail with your own efforts and abilities. Through this journey of independence and acts of faith you will develop the qualities and capability of self-sufficiency and with them honor and much success.

7. Trust is developed through the consistency of one's devotion, the status of one's relationship with another, and an esteemed reputation. There are many levels of trust the highest being the freedom to know and indulge in all the affairs and possessions of the confident trustor. Indeed many tests and trials must be administered and passed before trust may be awarded.

8. Those who speak with authority gain attention, and many will comply with their demands or suggestions. Those who receive such reverence should be kind, and respectable and have good intentions for those who accept and submit to their ideas.

9. Be sure to fulfill every promise you make and mean what you say. Your word is a contractual bond and whether you fulfill it or not it will have its effect.

10. Doubt, discouragement, and impatience destroy the energy of hope and hinder the bounteous flow of prosperity. However, the force of faith will always overpower words of doubt and diminish discouragement.

11. Triumph over anger and you will master self, patience, and order.

12. If you apply optimistic deeds and the energy of hope to those things that seem impossible to bring to fruition you are encouraging the ever-occurring miracles of faith.

13. Conceal your good deeds and others will make them known. Reveal the good that has been done to you and this will encourage the progression of favor.

14. Those who are truly grateful accept and give thanks even for those gifts that are less than desirable and treat them as ones of great value. This should be your attitude towards life every day you awake.

15. A considerate and mannerly person manages others' property with great care and are more cautious with others' belongings than they are with their own. Consider this, if you damage your own property it will be a loss, but if you damage someone else's property you may acquire a debt.

16. Your words are like fruit, make them sweet and others will take and use the good they produce. However, if they are bitter and distasteful no one will come to gather what you have to offer.

17. It is a grand and noble act to defend the lame and innocent, yet a great light shines in the heart of those who give generously to those in need. To make someone smile and invoke the presence of joy is to give a gift sent from heaven.

18. Those who provide and care for the lives and well-being of others more than they care for their own are the true guardians and leaders of the world.

19. If one is willing to place others in harsh or life-threatening situations then he or she should also be able to perform and

endure the burden they impose on others. A wise leader will send others to do only what he or she has done or would do themselves.

20. Because one has the ability or power to perform certain acts does not mean those acts should be carried out. All authority and activities must be applied responsibly and with extreme consideration.

21. Unjust authority controls the feeble-minded, oppress the less fortunate, invokes fear, imposes and enforces unfair rules, punishes unjustly, exploits sovereignty, and does whatever it desires. Whoever is wise and able to regulate the affairs and stability of many people responsibly with prudence is capable of establishing an affluent and jubilant nation and constitute permanent prosperity. Which of you are just and virtuous in all your ways?

22. A person who resorts to criminal acts to defend or provide for his or her family must receive punishment for the offense and justice for the cause in which the act was carried out. Justice must weigh the factors of all circumstances surrounding the incident and judge rightly to determine the penalty for the crime and a remedy that will assist the family.

23. The wicked may convert and become righteous just as the upright may change and become immoral. It's a matter of choice and the moral regard of one's conscience.

24. Confession is the only redress that may free one's conscience from guilt, reclaim the peace of one's soul and restore one's spiritual purity. To receive this purification one must openly repent, accept the discipline resulting and acknowledge the wisdom in refraining from repeating those acts.

25. Forgiveness is not always an easy deed to perform and only the merciful and compassionate are able. This wonderful act is

a cleansing to the soul and removes a great burden from the heart of those who truly desire to expunge their guilt.

26. What you reveal is what you want to be seen and what you conceal you desire to be hidden. Many are selfish and desire to possess all, while others are liberal and have nothing to hide.

27. Be sure of who you depend on, for many are not faithful nor willing to sacrifice and devote their time, efforts, or resources to assist you. However, you should always accommodate those who come to you for anything.

28. A kind and caring person will show favor with faith that good will derive from their deeds. However, those who are vainglorious shun the hopes and efforts of others striving to achieve. The faith-filled understand that faith is the source through which all things are manifested and realized.

29. To assist or advance others in the attainment of prosperity is the most glorious act any person can perform. Such a person shall be remembered and revered as a prestigious succor.

30. Those who respond with sympathy are kindhearted and merciful. Such a person shall wear a crown of honor and receive many blessings.

31. Those who use pity as a vice to acquire sympathy seldom receive it. It is wiser to acquire assistance with dignity and confidence.

32. Envy comes from those who are not content with their status or circumstances and acknowledge others who are doing or have achieved something worthwhile. Be cautious not to gloat in the presence of such people or their begrudging will turn into hatred.

33. Envious people are vexed when they see others obtain what they have not. It is not wrong to desire what others have,

however, it is wrong to envy them for having achieved or received what it is they have.

34. To accuse is an indication that there is no trust. Without trust, there is no unity, and without unity, there can be no harmony.

35. With quality condition is the focus point. For many, the slightest flaw can make even the most exquisite entity undesirable.

36. The very act of paying conscious attention to the internal and external parts and functions of your body instead of leaving them on autopilot will greatly reduce the process of aging and prevent disease. To sustain excellent health and maintain a purified body you must evaluate and regulate what you ingest as well as your physical activities. From there you will be able to perceive and aid the issues of your strengths and weaknesses.

37. One must be able to grieve without losing perspective of all the good that remains. Learn to overcome hardships by stimulating and producing the presence of joy, blessings, positive energy, and a renewed, exhilarating spirit. Every burden must be resolved by one's acceptance of the bounteous grace of life.

38. It is right to spend time with a friend, but you should not allow a friend to use your time for anything less than what is substantial or productive to your development.

39. Speak truth to those who deserve it, and it is better to remain silent than to tell a lie.

40. Only fools will allow themselves to be seized without doing so for a great cause. One is not a coward because he or she flees from danger, surely those individuals are wise. Yet even in the presence of danger one must not be timid.

41. Those who provoke or partake in violence are incapable of organizing and upholding true peace. Only to prevent or defend against an attack should there be such a reaction.

42. You will experience different emotions for a number of reasons. The key to a sound mind and tranquil spirit is to suppress those emotions and thoughts that may cause you any kind of stress or discontent.

43. It is better to be at peace learning and contemplating wisdom than it is to waste your strength, time, and resources chasing the entities and concepts of recurring trends. Those who are materialistic are passionately attached to what they possess and exhaust their finances and energy in an incessant and painstaking attempt to prevail over the inevitable process of obsolesce.

44. You will either experience and endure the difficulties and hardships of life or gain the wisdom to perceive and avoid what causes them.

45. There are times you will encounter things exhibiting the appearance, features, qualities, and essence of what you desire. However, as you inquire and engage you may notice many things are not what you were or are truly anticipating. Your search to attain the true essence of what you really desire must entail thorough scrutiny and a detailed evaluation which may require a great deal of time and effort. You should know precisely the status, qualities, features, and complete essence of what you desire so that when you find something resembling what you are searching for it will be as exact as possible to what you envision.

46. To have perfect knowledge of the future, complete understanding of the fathomless past, comprehension of every miraculous phenomenon, and to be irrepressibly powerful are the true and greatest desires of humanity. Seek and strive as

you may, only those who endeavor to achieve divinity shall attain such enlightenment.

47. Take heed! From one thought to the next the mind leaps and clings to whatever gains its attention. Even now your mind is under the influence of an outside force, doing with it whatever it pleases, soaking it with its concepts and ideas and pulling it deeper and deeper into its will and further and further away from your independent thoughts. How fragile the mind, so easy to sway and lead away from focusing on its true purpose.

48. To acquire the best is to retain the highest quality of prosperity and prestige. Treat yourself and others with the finest attributes of life, wealth, and prominence which will impress even you beyond arousal. You should always have in abundance so that you may be generous with the capacity of your benefaction.

49. You can be sure only of your own faith, hope, efforts, aspiration, and abilities. Everyone else may doubt and falter and even you may fall short of faith if you waver in uncertainty. Teach yourself to stand firm, strong, dutiful, and confident. For you are your primary source for success, prosperity, and happiness.

50. At the core of every machine, enterprise, or productive movement lies a powerful and imaginative mind. There is always an opportunity to contribute to the efforts and success of groundbreaking innovations, and to leave your unique mark on the world. By tapping into your innate creativity and striving to bring fresh ideas and perspectives to the table, you can make a meaningful impact on the world around you and play a vital role in shaping the course of human progress.

XI

SECTION ELEVEN

1. A dedicated student seeks to learn the master's greatest secrets, while an inattentive and uncommitted student risks missing out on the most valuable teachings and the wisdom to excel and attain mastery.

2. The wise student hears the master's voice even when he is not in his presence. He remembers every decree and his actions are always in accord with the master's instructions.

3. To study one must be still and attentive. To practice one must be actively engaged and consistent.

4. What the masters are most concerned with regarding their students are their devotion, their determination, their ability to heed instructions, their willingness to practice incessantly, sacrifice greatly, persevere sufferably, and most importantly their unfaltering loyalty.

5. The masters discipline their students with an iron rod when they wish to instill in them strength, correction, exceptional abilities, and wisdom. They show no mercy though all their

actions and judgments are just and they themselves righteous, kind, and merciful.

6. The master is prepared, he knows his purpose, he does not pollute his mind nor his body, he maintains harmonious order and gives wise and admirable counsel. The master's primary objectives in life are to become compleat and unparalleled in all the meaningful acts, elaborate his infallible essence, and achieve his grand state of divinity. His territory is safe and secure, his surroundings are in immaculate condition, he never angers, and is always calm and at peace. The master's principal rules in life are to love and care for all.

7. To become a master you must endure the sacrifice of self and worldly desires, understand the purpose of those sacrifices, and constantly develop new strengths and abilities that will produce in you higher levels of disciple and incisive faith. Study these things and you will acquire the mind of the masters and perfect the ideals and supreme goal of the true path.

8. There is a path that will take you speedily to your desired destination. However, many choose a path that strays and takes them far from where they need to be. Perceive and remain focused on the path of purpose, passion, and prosperity and you will establish yourself where you truly desire to be.

9. Be where you are knowing and preparing for where you desire to place yourself. Using the full measure of your faith and mind, you must perform with purpose and advance with diligence.

10. Go within and you may discover, bring out and reveal what you give attention to, and manifest and display the essence of what has been instilled in your mind and incites your actions. All things brought to the mind now dwells within.

11. Look within and you may realize your true nature, perceive what it is you truly desire, and discover what your personality

is really like apart from what you express and reveal to others. Go within and you may see what no one else can see until you willingly or inadvertently expose those intimate characteristics you keep concealed.

12. The moment you gain a person's attention and get them to respond to you, you put them in a conscious trance. The more you indulge in their personality the more their true characteristics will be revealed and eventually you will begin to tap into their subconscious mind, gradually gaining knowledge of their true nature, motives, and desires. If you are confident, competent, and intriguing enough to sustain their attention, you may get them to open up to you in a way that will allow you to influence and persuade them to comply with your will.

13. No one may profess to what he or she has not experienced personally. Without encountering the realities of an actual event, one is merely speculating ideas of how those events may have occurred or may be experienced. Until one has encountered every aspect of an event personally it is unwise of that person to assume, judge, or think he or she actually understands.

14. You create circumstances by giving or not giving attention to what is going on in and outside of your environment. Knowing this the wise establish themselves in safety far from the concepts, entities, and substances of entropy.

15. Every word is in itself a source of power and a dynamical and virtual essence that you may use to incite events. However, the ability to carry out the purpose for which one's words are invoked lies within the knowledge, power, authority, and status of the one invoking them.

16. Humanity's awareness and reliance upon the existence of materialism has brought about their reasoning and understanding of reality as they now perceive it. Humanity's ability to reason is superb and they have acquired a great deal

of knowledge attributed to the universe and its symmetries. However, because of their tight hold on worldly concepts and material possessions humans have reduced their ability to achieve universal perception and have greatly diminished their chances of realizing their state of divinity which would endow them with the power to regulate and facilitate the order of the universe. There are many truths and realities with unorthodox dimensions that humanity has blocked their minds from perceiving, discovering, or being able to comprehend. You, as an intelligent being, are obligated to excel and exceed beyond the presence of all limitations.

17. To free your essence from being chained to the essence of the world you must release the notion of every worldly concept from your mind and achieve a mental state of clarity and renewal. Such a feat requires deep meditation, and if you acknowledge the earth as a very tiny entity within an exponentially infinite and unconscionable universe you will achieve this goal and acquire the mental and spiritual clarity that will allow you to imagine, devise and enter realms and realities unfathomable by those bound to objectionable circumstances and customed ideologies. Ponder this; many are circumscribed to a life of ignorance and perpetual stagnation.

18. It is better to know than to see, for in knowing one's prospects are realized.

19. The brain is confined to the body, but the spirit and mind are free to journey beyond all realms, realities, and limitations. Use these dynamic faculties to transmute your body and spirit into whatever essence you desire to fashion.

20. Those who acquire true enlightenment of self understand I am us, meaning he or she realizes the presence of all people as one body and does not imply material possessions as mine, but rather all things as ours. This selfless achievement requires inner peace, true knowledge of self, faith in unity, and complete detachment from all material possessions.

21. You attract the experiences and things you have by acknowledging and accepting what you believe constitute and consummates the attributes of reality. If you are able to perceive the many verities of life you may better understand your existential disposition and order many realities to adhere to your vision.

22. Behind the perception and ideas of one's mind are the entities and activities that gains and holds its attention and influence its conceptual beliefs. Nothing is encountered, observed or incites an intellectual reaction except that which captures and stimulates the mind.

23. The laws and principles that bind you to your circumstances are truly within you and sustained or changed chiefly by you. Indeed the stations and conditions you experience are attained, shaped, fortified or altered by the things that influence you. And how you perceive and respond to those influences create the effects of your circumstances. One thing is certain; you will always have options and many aspects of realities to consider.

24. You will encounter many spirits and places on your journey through life, therefore, remain alert so that when you do encounter a place, a living being or a phantom spirit within an entity such as this book, you will be able to perceive the nature, conduct, activities and objectives within as well as the nature and intentions of your own presence and motives. When you enter a place, give attention to, or entertain yourself with those entities or living beings, you must realize you are allowing them an opportunity to influence you and bind their essence to yours. Be wise so you may see plainly and know exactly what you may attract and attach to your essence if you choose to become involved with these things. For even this book is an entity with an active influential objective that is now forever a part of your soul.

25. Create an ideal model for your mind and fill it only with those concepts and activities that will form and solidify the mind-set and realities you desire. Your supreme objective should be to build for yourself a life comprised of knowledge, wisdom and power.

26. The fount of life is affluent and eternally active. To partake in this eternal convention you must discover and utilize the elements, activities and energies perpetuating vitality and the productions of vigor. Search vehemently for knowledge beyond that of human intellectuality.

27. Those who borrow provisions are not self-sufficient or satisfied with the quality of their status. The things they want exceeds their mental or physical faculty and are greater than what their abilities will allow them to attain. Until they've paid back their debt their lender will own a part of their essence.

28. Sometimes the things you desire are not acquired or cannot be fulfilled because you have either not developed enough to retain them, you are not in an appropriate position to receive and sustain them, or you have enhanced your essence or status and are too great to attend to them with adequate attention.

29. If you seek wisdom you will learn to protect yourself against the destructive forces of entropy and the many fatuities carried out throughout the world. Before you can receive such enlightenment you must acknowledge and understand the things you've attracted and have made a part of your life and remove or remedy what has or may cause you to suffer or burden you with any kind of stress. It is imperative that you protect and strengthen your physical, intellectual, and spiritual essence frequently.

30. There is much you do not have knowledge of or access to that causes you to accept and live with the concepts and realities you've embraced. Look deeper into all matters and the

ways in which those around you are living and you may discern your presence and status amongst them.

31. What you see but did not create comes from an intellectually productive source. Find that source and there is another creative source responsible for the creation of that source. The important issue is what these sources and their creators manifest and why, and what you will do with your knowledge of each of those sources.

32. To be the source that manifests and sustains the provisions, conventional development, and objectives of others you must establish your facilities with great authority, have a powerful sense of leadership, avoid the common perceptions and edicts of the masses, and innovate the prospects, resources, and means of operation for society. Achieve this status and many will seek your essence and strive to sustain a lasting bond with you.

33. If you are a massive source of positive energy, pure thoughts, and healthy habits, you will be able to restore life, stimulate joy, and give perfect health and wisdom to others. Energize your miraculous healing power by being forever youthful, robust, compassionate, faith-filled, and a potent spirit infused with a mind of love and enough confidence to perform miracles.

34. With all that you desire to achieve or receive know that from the moment the idea is conceived in your mind your faith activates your attractable energies to accomplish the objective. If you believe and sustain an attitude of competence and an absolute will to succeed, your desire will be realized. Your accomplishments depend entirely on the measure of your faith.

35. As soap is used to clean the body, so one may cleanse and strengthen the spirit by applying the mind regularly and extensively to the divine scriptures and teachings of the masters.

36. By constantly contemplating, working on, and reiterating the thought seeds planted in your mind you are providing the mental stimulus required to produce and develop the essence of the things you give attention to. Monitor your cognitive activities attentively and you will have the advantage of good fortune and exceptional success.

37. Believe this to enhance your spiritual awareness; you will perceive your divine presence, acknowledge your true purpose, and achieve the full essence of your preternatural being.

38. When all is well everyone seems to be caring and trustworthy. However, when trials, temptations, and hardship arise many abandon, betray or become dishonest. When someone claims to be faithfully devoted to you, you must put them to the test. Those who remain faithful at your side, regardless of how burdensome the hardship or enticing a temptation through the entire trial, deserve your unbroken trust and loyalty in return.

39. The greedy are insatiable. If they take from others unjustly or unfairly, they will lose more than they've gained through the mysterious events of karma.

40. Functionalism and divinity should be the central points of your thoughts. Knowing this, it is wise of you to seek out and embrace the teachers of wisdom. Take this path and you will discover the greatness of life and realize just how significant, creative, and fortunate you truly are.

41. Wisdom is hidden from foolish and lackadaisical individuals, and the path leading to it is much too difficult for them to find. It requires much discipline to accept and practice the teachings of the masters.

42. If you choose to enter the path of righteousness you will realize the secrets of life belong solely to those with wisdom

and understanding, and that it is these few who can teach you and reward your sincere and diligent pursuit for divinity.

43. A fool is not someone with a mental disability but one who is unwilling to acknowledge right from wrong and noble from ignoble and choose the latter.

44. It is better to give thanks with a pleasant gift or a helpful deed than to simply say thank you. Show that you are grateful, and you will be remembered.

45. A pure and uncorrupted mind may be trained to acquire exceptional skills and divine knowledge. However, those whose minds are tainted and given over to sin, degrading concepts, and the common ideals and conduct of social inanities are subject to impure thoughts, foul habits, and vile entertainment.

46. If you believe yourself worthy you must teach and inspire others who have not acquired the wisdom to perceive the supreme importance of life and nobility. Those who revere and honor the ideals of God are lights of the world and many will perceive this glorious essence upon them.

47. Grace is having been given what you have not acquired on your own and gratitude is being grateful for the blessings you receive.

48. Work to develop a fortified and comfortable home, study to become intelligent, invest in the endeavors of prosperity, volunteer to advance humane ideals and conditions, and travel to experience and enjoy the many wonderful places of the world. This is the way of life for those who are driven to prosper and live happily.

49. Every adolescent should be given over to extensive training, tribulations, and acute studies. Discipline must be instilled through industrious feats to insure that they possess

the courage, knowledge, determination, self-confidence, vigor, and noble qualities attributed to those men and women who are notably exceptional.

50. The power of prayer infuses faith, relieves the pressure of heartaches and burdens, refreshes and revives the spirit, impels strength, induces new hope, and suppresses fear. Through earnest prayer and faith in the presence of divinity, you will receive comfort, wisdom, and new opportunities to increase your understanding and enhance your perception to perceive many aspects of life.

XII

SECTION TWELVE

1. For attaining discipline, for understanding the teachings of enlightenment, for giving prudence to the young, and knowledge and insight to the untaught, let the discerning add to their learning, for understanding proverbs, parables, and epigrams of the wise.

2. If you accept my words and store up my teachings within you, turning your eyes and ears to wisdom and applying your heart to understanding, then you will consummate the ways of the masters and hear the voice and commission of God.

3. As the wise give wisdom through their deeds, so the words of their mouths bring knowledge and understanding.

4. Do not forget my teachings but keep them active in your heart, for they will secure your path and bring you into a life of great prosperity.

5. Do not allow love and faithfulness to leave you; lock them around your neck and write them on the fabric of your soul.

Then you will win favor with the masters and a good name in the assembly of men.

6. Acquire prudence, strive for understanding, and do not forsake wisdom or swerve from these teachings, for they will protect you and cause you to excel in freedom and righteousness.

7. Wisdom is imperial, therefore, gain wisdom. Though you may give up all you have, pursue enlightenment and embrace understanding.

8. I give you enlightenment, expose wisdom, and lead you along the true path. Hold on to my instructions and do not forget them; uphold and express these teachings with your life.

9. Do not set foot on the path of evildoers or partake in the activities of those who are idle. Avoid sin and perfect your path of prosperity.

10. Let your eyes search for wisdom and do not change your objective. Make straight paths for your feet and take only those ways that shine with the glory of virtue and knowledge.

11. Whoever corrects those who gibber invites insult. However, if you advise one who is wise he will become even wiser.

12. Ill-gotten wealth decrease in value, but righteous hands produce honorable endowments.

13. The deeds of the righteous are infrastructures of love, compassion, and prosperity, but violence and greed drive the spirit of those who are callous.

14. The wise store up knowledge and benefactions for those in need, but the deeds of fools incite corruption and destruction.

15. The wealth of the wise ensures a fortified life, but poverty is the consequence of those who fail to seek wisdom.

16. He who instills disciple enriches the lives of others with purpose. Those who fail to heed his teachings will find themselves constantly burdened with distress.

17. Those who express and promote hatred will dwindle into a pit of revolting darkness; they are carriers of the worse disease.

18. When an evil-minded person speaks sin and perversion are afoot, but the words of the godly puts them to shame and outshine the evil they exert.

19. When those of immoral disposition rise to a state of prominent status, many who proclaim to be virtuous will revere them. Ignoring the virtues and righteous ideals of God, they honor those whose speech and conduct are demoralizing.

20. Those who are evil will be consumed by its destructive force, but the righteous will bloom and flourish like the spiritual garden of Eden. What the wicked dread will overtake them, but what the godly desire will be received.

21. If the rich perceive the poor and do nothing to enhance their financial and educational status they will never understand the mind and spirit of God. Let the poor feel blessed and show them the way to prosperity.

22. The virtuous and those who turn to divinity will elevate in moral integrity, but evil-doers are openly profane, their speech and actions filled with the impurities of sin. Such individuals invoke malign omens causing great spiritual degradation to many souls.

23. What good is all your work, prayers, and studies if you haven't learned to fill the minds, hearts, and spirits of others with love, joy, faith, and prosperity?

24. When pride enters a man's spirit he thinks of himself as one greater than others, becomes presumptuously vainglorious, slights the presence of others, and disregards the moral objective.

25. A kind man gives freely with no alternative motive. In doing so he benefits himself and reaps a sure reward. The selfish wonder why he is so revered.

26. Through the deeds of the just and noble a nation excels in prosperity, amity, and unity, but the ways of the callous and egocentric are pretentious and surreptitious. They build a nation with many prisons, dubious legalities, and citizens who are misgoverned and restless.

27. Whoever embraces discipline and diligence enjoys life, but those who despise the practice of orderliness must endure the effects of hardship, stress, and chaos.

28. The ways of the fool seem right to him, but when he finds himself in trouble he complains and places blame on others.

29. The wise, if wealthy, have no desire to live extravagant lives or collect and amass material possessions for themselves. They understand it is more valuable to use their surplus proceeds to help those impoverished.

30. A fool shows his annoyance at once, but a wise man proves he is temperate.

31. The dexterous mind engages in the conduct of business and endeavors of profound achievement, but those of lesser ambition remain laborers.

32. The imprudent inherit adverse fate, but the wise are fortunate in many endeavors.

33. The folly of a fool is his prominent crown, but the wisdom of the wise is a wealthy estate.

34. Educational faculties are the havens of intellectual profluence, accessibility, and gratifying comfort. However, the uneducated will find it difficult to attain benefactors, valuable resources, empowerment, and more desirable stations in life.

35. Success loves preparation as pursuance admires resilience.

36. Enthusiasm prepares the path for achievement, but pessimism extrudes an air of doubt and defeat. Embrace and increase your faith for success.

37. Those who do what they know is injurious to others are brave when they are out of the sight of authority, but when justice arrives they run, hide, and attempt to conceal their deeds.

38. A simple man believes and accepts anything, but a prudent man perceives the truth and significance in all things.

39. Every situation and consequence bound to you is yours to manage. If you accept responsibility you will perceive all the effects of your actions and learn to order your destiny.

40. To discover the elements, laws of physics, and life beyond earth great feats and tremendous sums of money are invested in theoretical experiments, yet the poor are reduced to poverty and left in a state of degradation. Humanity must be your first and most significant priority before striving to fathom God's creative faculties. Ponder this, why should you possess knowledge of the many dynamics, dimensions, or other intelligent beings of the universe if you cannot devise a way to establish a harmonious and prosperous union with your own kind? God's particles and the vast cosmos will sustain themselves while you invest in your most intelligent advisers and spare no expense on what your greatest feat should be,

which is to help those who struggle to find or sustain a comfortable home and joyful life. I can only imagine what you would do to my world and race if we were to enlighten you with the knowledge of all that we possess.

41. He who oppresses the poor shows contempt for all of humanity, but whoever is good to the poor honors the ideals of God.

42. There are those who experience or see injustice but have no power to reprimand those committing the offense or change circumstances, and those with the authority to rectify such issues. Where there is corruption, you can be sure those in power are aware, choose to renounce responsibility, and refuse to correct the injustice of those situations.

43. Enter the circle of the undisciplined and you will emerge a simpleton. Enter the assembly of the wise and you will emerge with superior intelligence and success allotted to a select few.

44. The greatest achievement consists in the attainment of a true state of sovereignty and the industrious facilities of autonomy.

45. A fool cannot perceive nor understand the mental and physical diligence that goes into building, sustaining, and safeguarding a civilized society and viable economy. He unwittingly depends on the service of the government, does nothing to contribute to its development, and complains about how much better things should be.

46. Though there are times you may not feel appreciated or acknowledged as worthy of the earnest deeds and attention of others, you must value the principles of self-esteem and hold others in high regard. Remember, love and compassion are the most significant attributes of the golden rule.

47. To perceive life as a miraculous and divine gift and to treat it as such is the divine enlightenment and principles taught throughout this book. Heed these sacred teachings and wisdom will come to you and guide you to the temple of the divine masters.

48. To attain true enlightenment and a refined mindset one must possess these great virtues; morality, altruism, self-disciple, divine wisdom, diligence, the practice of meditation, the pursuit of great aspirations, absolute truth, autonomy, unbigoted love, and placidity.

49. Find this esoteric sect and you will discover the mystical codification of all truths.

50. I speak a message among the mature, but not the wisdom of this era or of the authority of this age who disregard the ideals of God. I speak, however, of God's secret wisdom, a wisdom that has been hidden within us, destined for our divinity from the beginning.

WISDOM EXPOSED

SECTION TWELVE

THE TWELVE DIVINE RULES OF THE MASTERS

1. Be wise and practice the ideals of the masters.

2. Protect your conscience and do not join in with those who indulge in foul habits or seek to do wrong.

3. If you can perceive and avoid immorality, do your best to teach others to do the same.

4. Practice the arts of discipline, meditation, and nobility.

5. Strive to make every area of the world a place where God would feel comfortable residing. Keep the earth clean, healthy, holy, and fruitful.

6. Do not give your mind and attention to frivolous entertainment and unproductive activities. Instead focus on the advancement of prosperity, enlightenment, and betterment of humanity.

7. Keep yourself from being attached to worldly ideals and develop a stature of sovereignty.

8. Practice becoming a healer, altruist, and thaumaturgist. This is the highest path of spirituality and the enlightened route of the masters.

9. Maintain your health and the order and conditions of your life and assist others with this process as well. This is the way of oneness and second to the greatest commandment.

10. Believe in the ideals of God, pray to receive them, strive to embody this spiritual essence, and give thanks for your being.

This is how you will acquire the secrets of heaven and achieve divinity.

11. Obey the teachings of the masters, become a student of the Mystery School, and commit to becoming one of the prominent teachers of divinity.

12. Pursue the elusive yet invaluable virtues of love, joy, extravagance, harmony, knowledge, and prosperity. Aspire to live a purposeful, exquisite, and wholesome life as you practice these teachings.

ESOTERIC TERMINOLOGIES

The Beginning - The point when the divine beings summoned the primary material elements and set in motion the earliest events that shaped the universe.

Any fleeting moment or significant occurrence that transpires in the boundless expanse of time.

The threshold through which every conceivable reality is born, emerging from the ethereal realm of Nothingness.

Divine Light- Enhanced consciousness of one's divine presence, emphatic faith, creative power, and freedom to conceive, construct, and manifest realities from the unbounded expanse of the Realm of Nothingness.

The accumulation and infusion of relevant information and material properties that are imperative to induce the phenomenon of realism.

Divine Spirit- The transcendent essence of life which comes as intelligent spiritual beings possessing the ideals of God to assist and enlighten those striving to achieve their state of divinity.

Nothingness- The phase where all creative power is generated, the tectonic elements of creation are hyper-physically induced and every idea conceived may be materialized, mechanized, and exserted upon the Realm of Realism.

Where the manifestation and true presence of any entity acquires its essence and is deliberately or inadvertently invoked by a conscious being or beings.

A perfect state of tranquility and emptiness.

Present yet indefinite and exhibiting no meaningful or valid purpose.

Overstand- To have knowledge and understanding of present or eventual realities and positioning oneself so that one is not affected or overpowered by such events, entities, or forces and may utilize those realities to one's benefit.

Sovereign Being- One who has established him or herself in a state of autonomy free of all government legalities and society's conventional activities.

A person of true freedom who has effectively established a perpetual life-enhancing matrix of functionalism.

One who has attained supreme enlightenment pertaining to industrial enterprising and has acquired power and true authority over any number of territories and commercial or political facilities.

One with intellectual ingenuity, creative freedom, and eminent independence.

State of Divinity- The stature and power of a divine being who can readily transmute, embody any form or essence, and induce phenomenons.

Having a sublime essence and godlike abilities and powers.

True Path- The path of righteousness and wisdom in which one who accepts the ideals of the masters and strives to achieve their state of divinity must live.

An exceptional lifestyle achieved through unwavering reverence to the ideals of divinity, righteous living, incessant acts of kindness and compassion, and a readiness to teach and empower others with these ideals.

A teaching which enables one to enter the Realm divine beings.

ORDER OF BEINGS (6)

God- The highest ideal of a sovereign divine being with superlative power and abilities.

The Great Spirit.

Divine Masters- Faithful subordinates to the Great Spirit.

Divine Beings- Demigods who were once sub-divine beings and through divine meditation and spiritual ascendance have achieved their state of divinity.

Master- An enlightened teacher of the ideals of divinity and the true path.

Anyone who is highly knowledgeable and remarkably competent with the ability to perform proficiently or teach the attributes, functions, purposes, and required skills of any subject, art, craft, or entity.

Sub-Divine Beings- Humans or other high-minded intellectual beings.

Sub-Beings- Creatures (Animals and insects).

WISDOM EXPOSED

Coming in 2025

WISDOM EXPOSED 2

JUDGMENT OF ENDS

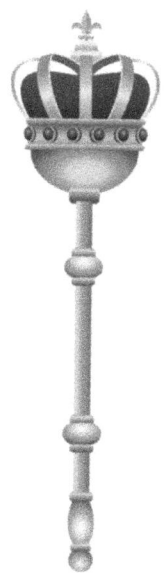

Ra-shieke Boyd

WISDOM EXPOSED 2

Preview

SECTION ONE

1. The penetralia of wisdom is discovered by few and even those who encounter it are perplexed by its inscrutable conundrums. Continue to search deeper, longing to fathom and ascertain what's hidden within the subject of wisdom and enlightenment will come to you and place you where you may see clearly the many agents of wisdom laboriously at work.

2. Regardless of sight and physical light many remain blind, unable to perceive, comprehend or understand. Indeed with their eyes they see, but without prudence and meaningful purpose, they walk about ignorant, without spiritual light in a world fraught with discomposure and confusion.

3. Elucidation comes to those with mental discipline who withdraw the senses from all trivial realities and concentrates the mind on attaining truths to the most obscured mysteries.

4. Rule yourself with an iron rod yielding to no temptation, giving your mind to lengthy edification, and the development of virtuous characteristics. Do this and you will discover a superb paradise exerting wonders beyond this realm and bestowing to you the most extravagant endowments.

5. Attend the mind as something to be affected; engage in feats of meditation exceeding your greatest application of cognitive development; muse the functioning presence in all aspects of

life; contemplate the events, realities, and circumstances of the ages; and journey to consult the masters. In this, you will attain true peace, devise perfect symmetries and realize the exploits of self-actualization.

6. The most significant occult, clandestine secrets, and uncharted dimensions of life are to those who know. Explore, examine, investigate, and study to ascertain knowledge and truth. This is how you will gain divine enlightenment and become one of the great masters of wisdom.

7. Enter here, the realm of meditation, and fill your soul with tranquility. Calm your spirit, give comfort to your mind, and your body to the energy of the universe. Effective indeed is the spiritual power adduced from a well-founded and substantified seance.

8. Look not for the physical essence but conjure the spirit. Presence is invoked by the faith in which it is earnestly believed. From here manifestation derives.

9. Think about these things then discern what it is you encounter. Truth is found only by those who are able to perceive beyond the conventional affairs of society.

10. Embrace the beginning and you will learn the components and acts of incitement. The key is to perceive the spiritual and physical connections and evolutionary processes in all structures and activities.

11. What something becomes is determined vastly by inferential discretion. Abstract is displaced by the synthesis of conception, from here the definitive is formed.

12. Fathom the notion of ignorance. We are here as a collective for one divine objective, therefore, let us not lose sight of it and forfeit this exceptionally rare phenomenon we call life.

13. When time has passed and the craving for worldly possessions ceases, this I hope you will live to see.

14. Strength increases strength, power influences power, and dominance conquers the venerable.

15. If you number your strengths against your weaknesses which will dominate? Destroy every weakness and you will wield the power to dominate any arena of contest.

16. Acknowledge your weaknesses, analyze and study them intently until you come to know all of them intimately. Be meticulous seeking many ways to change them into strengths, and practice excessively to forge them into indomitable attributes of power.

17. Indolence and ignorance are your most detested enemies. If you allow them to hold you in bondage they will reduce you to a state of unrelenting grief and baleful ordeals.

18. To suffer, to endure hardship, to persevere in self-discipline, to encounter misfortune and undergo unbearable grief; these will either break your spirit down to a decrepit and feeble state of disablement or forge upon your character knowledge, strength, and abilities indispensable to the masters.

19. Knowledge and prudence are the tools used to gain power. If you acquire and use them wisely you will submit to no entity, force, or limitation.

20. There is a radiant light even in total darkness for those who walk assuredly by faith and not by sight.

21. When the moving force and irrepressible determination of will come, fruition reveals its indubitable capabilities.

22. Do not become dependent on hope or chance, for they may deceive you and cause you unrest and the burden of disappointment.

23. Find the presence of peace, release every burden, and lock the mind in serenity. Be calm and you will find that every storm will pass.

24. Acknowledge your breathing, the beating of your heart, the beauty in nature, the easy flow of a stream, and the settled state of a stone on a mountain. Relax, become one with these and do as they do.

25. Resolve your issues with the most favorable advantage and move forward in your plans. When things fail rethink the purpose and strategy of your ideas.

26. Become active, engrossed, passionate, and untiring in your adventure for life and prosperity. Live and let nothing and no one deter or hinder your will.

27. Your will is what takes you wherever you go and cause you to do whatever you do. Keep a tight grip on your will and you will control the direction of your destiny.

28. Your actions exhibit your intentions more than your words. What you exert yourself to do is more powerful than what you say you will do with your words.

29. The wise work harder because they know that excellent performance produces better results and better results rewards of greater value.

30. When dominance is assumed and authority implied another is submissive, feels unequal, spiritually declined, and lacks the will and passion to command control over his or her own being. Many are taken and given over to oppression, drudgery,

and savagery because they have not acquired a sense of purpose or an identity that exerts confidence and power.

31. Those who are outwitted and overpowered will experience the effects of their failure to excel in intelligence, establish unassailable security measures, and develop a reliable capacity for knowledge. It is imperative that you secure your essence, station, and position with extreme diligence and trustworthy alliances.

32. Do not be seduced or overwhelmed by emotional influences or you will be enslaved to tantalization, sensualization and a profound desire to be accepted. Free and highly esteemed are those who do not succumb to addictions or fall to the controlling effects of seduction.

33. If those close to you abandon their devotion and respect for you, you must withdraw yourself from them and be on alert for acts of betrayal.

34. Even when we fail, are disappointed, lose faith, or feel defeated, truly we have become stronger. By tomorrow you will have developed into a wiser and more industrious individual.

35. Diligence, attentiveness, and practical application for advancement are key components in building a competent and stout character. Endure, overcome, and build your character to withstand any and every adversity.

36. Let the lackadaisical and those who are without definitive objectives sleep, play, and engage in the most trivial and inane activities. For they will inherit what the purposeful, intelligent, and those who live productive lives create, discard and leave behind.

37. When the zealous and those inclined towards things of higher importance impose rules and develop systems and

facilities with rigid guidelines for society to abide by, many become subject and soon lose the concept of individuality and the vital force of their sovereign capacity.

38. We see only the obvious of what is projected until we gain the wisdom to inquire and perceive the intrinsic nature and cryptic knowledge concealed within. The key to unlocking and perceiving these mysteries are discovered through the tedious process of investigative studies. The true value in beneficial realities are rarely conspicuous or easily understood.

39. You have to be fervently aroused, intensely productive, voraciously courageous, and vehemently eager to pursue and attain your highest aspiration. You will know when you are ready to pursue your greatest feat.

40. Use your mind actively to innovate, create, establish, and revolutionize new and better realities. Work emphatically to develop and enhance your status of prestige.

41. Prevent the mind from focusing on events eternal to the self and focus on evaluating your current state, your level of performance, and your ideal state. Self-perception allows you to see clearly every characteristic, habit, and condition of the person you are. You must, periodically, engage in the process of self introspection.

42. Through your ability to see what you are, how you behave, and your perception of all things, you will decide how you will represent yourself and how you desire to be perceived. This is your identity striving to idealize your perfect being.

43. People with strong achievement motives prefer objectives where skill rather than luck determines the outcome, seek social independence, have a future time perspective, high-level task performance, and lean toward the side of success. These individuals are usually disposed to entrepreneurship, personal responsibility, and reliability.

44. Basic ideals must be abandoned for the attainment of autonomy, sovereignty, and the great transcendence into divinity.

45. Identify the characteristics of one's spirit and you will possess the wisdom to know what he or she may or may not do. Indeed you may know the true nature of the soul if you perceive the objective of the spirit.

46. Be cautious and extremely mindful of those who do not strive for something of true value or have nothing to gain or lose. If that person engages you he or she may attempt to cause you stress, harm, or suffering.

47. If you can identify the nature of a person's soul you can either train it in a way that will allow it to become stronger and nobler or exploit it to make your soul stronger, wiser, and more refined.

48. When you incite or are lured into a situation you must be certain you can control and cause it to end with a desired result.

49. A calm and shrewdly guided mindset may advance with extreme accuracy and create or attain what is truly desired.

50. If you observe, it is not difficult to see that those lacking in wisdom are often susceptible to afflictions, unbecoming behaviors, foul habits, reprimands, unfavorable circumstances, and a failure to attain elevated levels of success.

WISDOM EXPOSED 2

SECTION TWO

1. With this tiny seed I sow in your mind a magnificent idea, one that shall take root and flourish. Believe in it, and I can assure you that success will follow.

2. To those who believe in the ideals of God, since they are in you, everything you desire you will receive. For the faith in which you believe in the ideals of God will be available to you in all you do and strive to realize.

3. Within the cognitive presence of every spirit lies a responsive force. This force is synthesized through the intellectual and physical exertions of each spirit, blending together the unique attributes of eventualities and the structural essence of what will be. To this end, you must form a superb ideal and establish a resolute commitment towards its realization.

4. We strive for something to come to pass, and when that thing has passed we strive for the next. The discerning are those who perceive their divine presence and comprehend the ultimate end.

5. We strive continuously to alleviate the overwhelming sense of purposelessness by fervently pursuing an endless array of endeavors. Thus, I urge you to work diligently towards attaining your state of divinity.

6. If you are stagnant and find it difficult to achieve a greater status or desired station how great is your mind or the

application of your efforts? There are many ways to achieve your greatest feat. The true objective is to discover and master all of those ways.

7. We may look to others to gain assistance and much will be given. Yet it is our own efforts, passion, and faith that we must rely on to make progress and accomplish our goals.

8. Society demands obligations and enforces liability as much as the universe demands progress and enforces order. Respect these and you will conceive the most exceptional ideals and be led into the most exquisite faculties.

9. How will prosperity and success come to you if you continue to put off the activities and tasks required to reach your goal? To fulfill your goal you must devise a pragmatic plan and put forth serious effort to bring it to fruition.

10. Acknowledge your aspirations, perceive the activities and facilities that will lead you in that direction, and see to it that you do not lose sight of it or are pulled in a direction that will take you off your path. Prosperity is the meritorious reward given only to those who pursue and achieve their highest aspiration.

11. It is better to develop and distribute products of the highest quality than it is to produce and dispense products of low quality. This practice will lead to the essence of quintessence and prove to be of the greatest quality when compared to like entities.

12. This very moment is the beginning! The first event in which you will consciously realize the power of inciting and manifesting many realities. Take advantage of your power to devise, actualize and create.

13. Intelligence requires a cannily mind upon which knowledge may be readily absorbed and easily retained. Create this

edifying fixation and you will encounter the manifestation of brilliant ideas, innovations, and creative inventions taking place all around you.

14. Every spirit or entity adapts to your spirit and moves in sync with the presence of your thoughts and faith. Through your acts towards your aspirations and the determination of your will to vitalize these ideas, all things work to produce resultant effects.

15. In all of your gains, losses, joys, and hardships do not forget to be grateful. Remember, when you came into life you brought with you nothing and if you take account you will see that you have much to appreciate.

16. All things were made to your benefit through those who sought to make life easier and more grandiose. However, many disregard these achievements giving their attention and life over to trivial activities and irrational fantasies.

17. It is not wise to put off consequential obligations, for this may lead to undesired liabilities and the loss of essential assets and personal property.

18. Do not delay in your responsibilities or you may find yourself overwhelmed by many incomplete errands or caught in the snares of debt and the inability to advance and succeed progressively.

19. To reach the apex of success you must inquire, seek wisdom, and gain knowledge. Be mindful of your destiny and what you pursue. By all means, avoid degradation.

20. A demonstration furnished with delightful amenities attracts many and stimulates aspiration. If you desire to gain attention this is a method that will easily draw it.

21. Pious thoughts and definitive actions lead to a life of good fortune and godliness. Indeed piety forges the path to true blessedness.

22. Diligence is the powerful engine that pushes beyond the boundaries of hope and achieves the success that mere desire is incapable of fulfilling.

23. The ability, will, and power to begin and follow through on a plan or the completion of a task are what success denotes. You will experience the joy, excitement, and rewards of your most outstanding accomplishments.

24. Look to the beginning and you will encounter the process of incitement as well as the most probable end. Perceive the components and attributes of incitement and you may gain the knowledge and power to mimic or incite your own process or dismantle the process of what you observe and desire to end.

25. Those who believe in death will surely encounter its silence, stillness, and complete darkness. However, those who believe in eternal life will remain forever vibrant in its aspiring and prevailing light.

26. It is not always easy to perceive yourself, the ways in which you conduct your behavior, your conditions, or the subsequential consequences of your actions. To see what you truly are you must be still, acknowledge your conditions, the events of your environment, what you did yesterday, what you plan to do today, and how you view and deal with the people you interact with every day. Do this and you will have a clear perspective of who you are, what temperament you are forging upon your character, and the realities surrounding the circumstances of your life.

27. To those who have not acquired a meaningful purpose to attribute to their life I say this. To excel and enjoy a productive life you must seek, find, and embrace subjects of edification,

vocation, and education. Engage and occupy your time with these and you will acquire a life filled with meaningful activities, enchanting events, and true happiness.

28. Refrain from partaking in veil practices and the controlling entities of addiction. A good and healthy life is made in high esteem, spiritual ascendance, pursuits of greater knowledge, and an increasing love of self.

29. There are many schools with any number of teachings. Become engaged by drawing from many subjects their edifying attributes and you will be knowledgeable and able to inform and educate others with information beyond their awareness.

30. From one need we determine another, and from one attainment we advance to the next. We strive constantly in pursuit of betterment desiring to facilitate our dominance over nature and the perfection of our greatest ideals.

31. With a few you may gain the attention of many. Gain the attention of many and your ideas will spread to the masses and become a cultural movement or social trend.

32. There is much to be accomplished and objectives that are not being attended that would greatly benefit the quest of our life's truest feats. Do not overlook what is supremely imperative to give attention to things that are trivial, or you will miss the grandiose end and never know why you are here.

33. To complete the process of self-actualization one must possess the propensity for engaging the faculties of education and higher learning.

34. Initially you must depend on the providence of the universe and develop the ability to become truly autonomous and self-operative. Indeed to acquire true life you must achieve your state of divinity.

35. To attain true enlightenment and a refined mind one must possess these great virtues; morality, altruism, self-discipline, divine wisdom, diligence, the practice of meditation, pursuing aspirations, absolute truth, autonomy, unbigoted love, and placidity.

36. Nothing comes to be that did not will itself to be, and nothing ceases to be that did not wish to suppress its being. All things adhere to their supernal purpose regardless of the direction anticipated. Things will and will not be how we think they should be.

37. Find this esoteric sect and you will discover the mystical codification of all truths.

38. Sit in silent meditation and you will purge the mind of all notions, concerns, and concepts. Now you may discover the realm of nothingness and encounter the superlative essence of divinity.

39. It is an excellent custom to pray and practice the ideals of God every day. In this state you will find that you are secure, protected, confident, and in the affluent grace of prosperity.

40. Relieve yourself of all desires and concepts. Here you will discover serenity, position yourself at the beginning, thwart the strenuous entanglement of any reality, and acquire those ideas that are instrumental to your transcendence.

41. If you become strenuously involved or attached to any reality you will be conceptually and emotionally actuated and, in some fashion, affected.

42. Your beliefs and the things in which you are involved reveals the attributes of what you've become. You must be sagacious with everything you give attention to.

43. When you acknowledge your position you must consider exactly how and what you've become.

44. An idea as small as a seed can grow to make you stronger and more successful or cause you to dwindle into a state of despair and disorder. For this reason, you should inculcate only those ideas that will produce the best rewards.

45. Pursuing success is like building a machine that serves a significant purpose and perpetuates an affluency of good fortune. See to it that the function of your mindset progresses with great efficiency and maintains a state of stability.

46. Methodological thinkers devise, create, and establish their path of success through the power of perceiving and pursuing the objective with true diligence and fantastical faith. This is a spirit driven to achieve its highest ambition.

47. There is much to be attained. Therefore, pursue what your heart desires and live with a sense of yearning and adventure.

48. Some things are better left alone. Engage them and you may incite events that you wish had not occurred.

49. What use is information if it is not intelligently applied? All the information in the world will not help those who lack the ambition and cognitive ability to facilitate conducive conditions and their most desired stations.

50. No matter how beautiful and exquisite the earth and all its wonders, you are so much more remarkable!

WISDOM EXPOSED 2

SECTION THREE

1. If you achieve a state of mental clarity all things will become transparent, and nothing will be hidden from you.

2. Incessant attention is given to those who are doing something intriguing with unwavering consistency. Devise such events and you will hold the attention and devotion of many for as long as you desire to keep them mesmerized.

3. The mysterious techniques of enchantment and elaborate rituals fascinate, capture the soul, and create deep spiritual effects. Such is the art applied to gain control over the mind and actions of others.

4. We empower, influence, and instill the beliefs and spiritual direction of others with our words and actions. Surely with encouraging words and good deeds you may be the cause of someone's achievements.

5. To charm and delight completely you must possess captivating qualities, an altruistic spirit, and the habitual practice of attracting, stimulating, and infusing the spirit, passion, and acquired ideals and interests of others.

6. Many people have no significant desires or do not know what they are seeking until someone plants an idea in their mind. Many aspirations, ideals, and acquired purposes are

attained through the words, actions, or accomplishments of others.

7. A unique and unrealized idea is brought about by those who look deep into the intrinsic and intricate features of certain ideas and perceive things that have not been perceived but can be created or arranged to adduce new features or unfathomed realities.

8. Ambition is like fire, filled with intensified and forceful energy. Those who have it are fervidly active and extremely proficient at pursuing every objective with the highest degree of certainty.

9. You will encounter those who talk about what they want or are trying to do, and those who do not speak of what they want to do but exhibit the direct manifestation of what they do. Only those avid pursuers of aspirations are filled with intensified ambition and possess the faith and energy to move through all obstacles, devise plausible strategies, and realize every one of their desires.

10. To incite motivation there has to be either an innate or acquired need or desire. This psychological drive encourages certain behaviors which arouse specific actions. When an incentive is formed a responsive process can ensure the effectuation of motivation.

11. The masters expect five high-minded qualities from their disciples. Indeed, we should all possess these characteristics; commitment to righteousness, competence, diligence, integrity, and high aspirations.

12. You will become what you are through the subjects and activities you are engaged with right now. Whatever you hope to be see to it right now.

13. Those who encourage you pour their spirit and faith into you. Use this energy to maximize the potential of your spirit and you will in turn strengthen their faith.

14. Success and achievements of the most exceptional aspirations go solely to those who can focus on devising a definitive plan and pursue its fruition with the greatest emphasis of attentiveness.

15. Your faith is a dynamic force energized by the resoluteness of your mindset. What you do exhibits your will being done.

16. It is good to know that we can always compound upon every situation or creation to perfect the essence of our greatest aspirations.

17. Your spirit needs a brighter light with less obscurity. For the greater your light the better you will be at perceiving and administering truths regarding the supreme purpose of life and the ultimate meaning and value of all things.

18. Realize what you want, and you will soon realize what you must sacrifice to receive it.

19. Life is yours, therefore you should make every issue pertaining to the livelihood, station, and condition of your being personal.

20. It is imperative that you search laboriously for all information that is and will be vital to your existence.

21. Many are driven or left in a broken world where their minds remain unfertilized and their spirits devoid of ambition and innovation. Such individuals can only be lifted out of this state by an incessant flow of inspiration, encouragement, relevant information, and compassion.

22. Unlock and energize the full potential of your mind and you will be free indeed. When pursued, success will come.

23. A person can be inspired by the words and speech of others to do what is right or wrong. Observe the speech and moral temperament of an individual and you will know whether he or she is deserving of admiration and great honors.

24. Examine the virtue and integrity of every spirit and associate yourself with those who uphold these characteristics to their highest standards.

25. Go to people, live with them, and learn all they know. Do this and they will accept you, and you will become a part of their circle.

26. Those who say it can't be done should not disturb or discourage those who are doing it.

27. However you find your attitude you will find the spirits, circumstances, stations, opportunities, and conditions of your life. With an optimistic attitude success, kindness, good fortune, and prosperity will come to you.

28. Every great achievement has certain components of operation, and every achiever becomes a master deviser of effective modes of action.

29. Never cease to strive for what you desire. Never behold life or your situation with a pessimistic attitude. And never let unfortunate circumstances lead you into wrongdoings. With a proactive mindset, you will perceive a world filled with numerous opportunities.

30. Since your expectations greatly affect your attitude, it is wise that everything you expect stimulates your motivation, ensures valid fruition, and reinforces a positive mindset.

31. Those individuals who believe they will succeed, win, or accomplish an exceptional feat are the ones who usually do. See to it that you possess this self-empowering spirit.

32. When the doubtful states the impossible, the faith-filled performs the miracle.

33. We are all influenced by others' attitudes, actions, beliefs, demeanor, words, status, and ideas whether they are good or bad. The goal is to make sure that you are in complete control of your temperament and realize how you will influence others.

34. You have within your spirit a supernatural ability that will allow you to control all things. This innate power awaits the force of your divine faith.

35. A strong belief system is not only protective and spiritually edifying, but a powerful generator of self-esteem. The better your belief system is equipped with strong morals, a disposition that encourages high quality, and a will to be proficiently competent and unwavering in faith, the easier it will be for you to establish and maintain a well-structured life.

36. If it can be envisioned it can be actualized, and if fervently pursued there is a heightened element of probability. Only through diligence are extraordinary realities faithfully pursued to the end.

37. The best experiences are to those who strive and work hard to encounter them. Greater success goes to the best of the best.

38. Devotion and commitment are the essential characteristics of those who are reliable. Only true fondness, admiration, and the deepest respect will meet the requirements of such loyalty.

39. All energy is built up and used towards a specific purpose. Be sure that purpose will produce a desired effect and provide you with a greater source of energy.

40. As you advance in knowledge, faith, abilities, and many endeavors you will find yourself in more ornate settings with better amenities and healthier living conditions.

41. Those who are extremely lackadaisical, don't have the ambition to work towards, and have no vision of achieving greater stations with better standards of living will make few and minor advancements, and settle into a state of permanent complacency.

42. Assistance will be given to those who work for it and are not afraid to ask. You must make your request with undoubting expectations.

43. When you aspire you must not doubt that you are equal to the task or unworthy of the rewards that come with the achievement.

44. We all live off each other's energies and ideas. Therefore, what is done and believed is likely to impact and affect us individually as well as a whole.

45. It is not the pulchritude of finely developed buildings, nor the stature and prestige of the noble or government council that makes a society great. However, it is the spirit and status of all the people within that reveals how a nation is to be regarded.

46. In a society that is financially burdened, has homelessness and crime, and experiences the indifference of gentrification you will also find governors and those in power who are incompetent in their positions like amateurs in the game of chess. They have no foresight and are unable to devise tactful strategies, and all their decisions are frivolous and discordant.

47. Though love is an emotion, feeling this way and that, its supreme objective is to ensure excellent health, encouragement,

adoration, protection, spiritual ascendance, and wholesome living conditions. Love is truly a lifelong process of devotion.

48. There is much to be gained and much to be lost. Determine what you are willing to lose and be sure what you gain yields a greater reward than your sacrifice.

49. Generosity expects and demands no recompense. For this, blessings are bestowed on the essence of the soul.

50. If you have a talent, you must find a way to exhibit and exploit it to your benefit. Those who allow their talents to go unnoticed will miss their opportunity to achieve their greatest aspirations.

WISDOM EXPOSED 2

SECTION FOUR

1. To perform a miracle there must be the presence of tremendous faith, a vacuity of doubt, and heroic confidence.

2. Consider the mind something to be undertaken. Muse, inquire, speculate, plan, devise, design, and resolve.

3. The future may be foreseen and structured to accord with one's prediction, yet such abilities require a sound mind with profound clarity, a heightened intuition, and a great capacity for awareness.

4. To gain the ability to see into all things you must first imply nothing, become aware of the obvious, and perceive and study that which is complex and obscure.

5. Practice and master the components of literature. Do this and you will become a proficient reader, an excellent chirographer, and an expert writer.

6. As you nurture the mind causing it to excel in wit you will discover the universe becoming a more elaborate realm with many exquisite amenities. Indeed it is a place of miracles and a true and absolute phenomenon of the mind.

7. For lack of divine knowledge many will suffer and die. For ignorance is the ultimate imputation of defeat, and misapprehension the primary cause of adversity.

8. With knowledge many will prevail, for correct and intuitive perception is the ultimate insurer of achievement and profound understanding the result of mysteries and correctness cerebrated.

9. The great mysteries of life are hidden from those who do not strive to discover the glories of this great phenomenon.

10. Ponder and pursue the five mysteries of life; the profundities of wisdom, truth, divinity, faith, and the Immaculate Spirit of God.

11. Like a self-thinking AI computer with a tremendous amount of information, so are those who are knowledgeable yet lack the mental ingenuity and conscious will to order and control the circumstances and direction of their lives.

12. In this reality called life you must make an inquiry of your presence, take note of what is truly essential to your life, and contrive to create, establish, and place yourself in your most favorable station.

13. Indeed you may laugh and enjoy the many fancies of life. But first, you must ensure your safety, establish your station and security, and make the providence of your sustenance infallible.

14. When the spirit is efficaciously moved by something influentially alluring, the body and mind will be motivated to produce the energy and ideas to engage and complete any undertaking.

15. An objective must be envisioned, a plan devised, and the activities required for fruition avidly pursued. See to it that the spirit is active, energized, and advantageously purposeful.

16. Every struggle or adversity is the result of the universe in its undeveloped state exerting its effort to help you achieve the perfection of your ideal state.

17. Being that you are one with the universe, if you learn to focus and control your mind you will master the ability to manipulate, order, regulate, and control all things.

18. Perceive and comprehend the energies and activities of the universe and whatever your aim it will be met with precise effectuation.

19. At this moment you must realize the fact that life as you have it exists solely through you, and that without you, it does not exist.

20. When those in high places go to those in lowly places with an earnest motive to do good, this is how they become great.

21. All aspirations are conceptual, achievable, and rewarded by true diligence. Thus, the fulfillment of a desire is acquired and kept.

22. It is the inner spirit and stimulated subconscious that creates the presence and essence of every entity, activity, and symmetry attributed to life. All things are consonant with the mind.

23. Blessed indeed are those who aspire to enrich the physical structure and spiritual essence of humanity. Empowerment and betterment will always create stronger and wiser beings.

24. Only by patience, faith, godly thoughts, unwavering diligence and continued importunity can one enter the temple of wisdom.

25. Only if the universe inside of you is greater than the universe outside of you will you see the big picture.

26. Put your trust in the light while you have it or you will succumb to the darkness.

27. Study diligently to understand the divine teachings and strive to discover your divine purpose and achieve your state of divinity. This way you will accompany me at the beginning.

28. Ponder this; the wise will always perceive the true value and deceptive objective in all things. Not all things are worth having or attending.

29. You must avoid being affected or influenced by people and things that do not pertain to your divine purpose, and if you are unable to master and prevail over such forces with true dominance you will experience and endure whatever fate those entities may impose and inflict upon you.

30. The true essence of life is impelled by the will and freedom to create, exert, and experience the presence of many phenomenal realities. With the will, anything can be done.

31. Truly inevitable are the exceptional expectations and unprecedented feats of those who align their essence and ideas with the nature and faith of God.

32. Those who live extraordinary lives have amazing views and the most exceptional ideals. Be sure to enter the circle of those who are intelligent, wise, adventurous, and prestigious. And so shall you be.

33. Every mind is similar to a treasure chest. Some possess great and valuable jewels, and others nothing of true value. See to it that your mind is one with the most elaborate and abundance of wealth.

34. Those with divine understanding can perceive the nature and truth in all things. Few words are needed for the wise to discern and determine what has happened or may occur.

35. You must pursue and persuade those you desire to endorse your objectives or assist you in your efforts without resistance. Indeed your mind is a powerful magnetizing force that can easily attract the people and resources required to achieve your goals.

36. Prepare yourself as best you can, pursue your hopes in spite of doubt, and continue in your objective until you've discovered the correct methods and proper applications required to realize your ambition.

37. If you've discovered what it takes to succeed and understand the process of prosperity, you've also discovered the path of comfort, serenity, and happiness. You are obligated to enlighten others and teach this path.

38. Motivate yourself to face and stand up to those challenges you think will be difficult and you will find yourself developing abilities, competence, confidence, and the results of proficiency.

39. Give your heart, mind, and greatest efforts to a meaningful objective. This mindset will lift you into a status and station in life with endless amenities and the presence of exhilaration.

40. To overcome and alleviate every form of stress or burden you must learn to order and control the circumstances of your life. Order and stability are acquired and maintained by those who are educated, financially secure, and manage all their affairs with prudence.

41. Do not cause harm or stress to others and be humble and cheerful with everyone you associate with. A wise and encouraging spirit is to others what fresh air and healthy foods are to the body.

42. Live today with your mind, eyes, and spirit focused on God, prosperity, success, and a gratifying future.

43. Believe in God, believe in heaven, believe in whatever great and extraordinary ideal that may exist in your mind. The first thing required to ascend is to believe.

44. If you have faith and desire to prevail in all things it would be prudent of you to choose what you believe wisely.

45. Every act whether good or bad comes from within the heart and it is what the eyes see and the ears hear that incites and develops the nature of the spirit.

46. If you are willing to believe you will come to accept the fact that your will is the most powerful force of life and life the miraculous creation of the will.

47. For fools there are many troubled days, but for the wise are many years of joy, peace, and prosperity.

48. Do only what is good in the eyes of God and bless others treating them as you would a beloved brother or sister.

49. Every person will in one way or another affect those who are somehow connected to them. However, a well-developed spirit will not be affected by those of negative intent because he or she remains fortified and nothing may dominate his or her mental and spiritual state.

50. Believe you are and strive to be the dominating force that will make life what and how you want it to be no matter how fanciful or exquisite your vision of that life may be. Thus, you will come to master your preternatural presence and divine power.

SECTION FIVE

1. What you intend to do is profoundly relevant to what will become of you.

2. To what you give attention, you will deposit into your mind, conduct your activities and invest in your future.

3. The greatest deed in life is to attend to those who are less fortunate. Whether with your time, finances, encouragement, or physical assistance, your kind deeds will help you to feel good and develop a better life for everyone.

4. The supreme goal of every government is to make life easier, more pleasant, enjoyable, safe, and comfortable for all its citizens and not just a few.

5. You will be as rich and happy as your spirit and ambition allow you to be, or as poor and depressed as your lack of motivation and understanding makes you.

6. You are an intelligent being and with this supreme power the universe will adhere to your commands.

7. Open your eyes and you may see what many believe; listen with thoughtfulness and you may gain the wisdom to discern what is true and right from what is deceptive and improper.

8. Insert your spirit into God's essence and you will become a living light of spiritual power and divine understanding.

9. Receive the spirit of God into your essence and you will live forever healthy, whole, and youthful.

10. Those who are afraid of being seen for what they do and do not want their acts exposed are certainly engaged in offensive conduct. Yet much of what is offensive is encouraged and acceptable to the masses.

11. Study and learn; inquire and search; devise and create; build and reconstruct; prevail and succeed; evolve and transcend. From one systematic scheme of social phenomena to the next, every generation ascends.

12. Look and observe and you will realize that others have devised and created what you see. Products of success abound in all that be. From this mind to the next, we transfer our achievements which are further advanced through the process of innovation.

13. Though the righteous are few, if they work together they could change the ways and unfortunate circumstances of many.

14. If by chance you encounter someone who is disabled or in need and requires assistance, it is wise and noble to aid them with your best effort. In doing so you will make your character one that is caring and a true recipient of great esteem.

15. Be on alert for danger and guard your life employing all means so long as they don't endanger others.

16. You were bestowed the superb attribute of intuition, be sure to enforce it and you will avoid many burdens and misfortunes.

17. There is something keeping your attention. Therefore, do not lose sight of your highest aspiration and forfeit the definitive objective. Never sacrifice great achievements for minor pleasures.

18. Those who are lazy and do not engage in endeavors with a fervid passion will not produce outstanding results or receive the great benefits of success.

19. Those who strive to be competent and proficient in every skill will become masters of their trades, and the benefits of their labor will multiply and lead to excess.

20. Being that faith is the essential force required to manifest those things that are not into things that are, it is a divine ability. Therefore, faith too can and must be exercised, facilitated, amplified, and mastered.

21. When a person is not happy and living a productive life, he or she will find it difficult to bring joy and positive energy to others. Until this person discovers meaningful and gainful work and makes him or herself joyful, he or she will experience and cause others to experience misery.

22. Consciously or subconsciously, your thoughts about almost everything are largely formed by preformed opinions and ideas fostered by the compelling methods of suggestion.

23. The fact of belief is that it influences your thinking and actions a great deal more than logic. Ratiocination is seldom the dominant process of thinking.

24. Most individuals place all their reasoning on what they do instead of what they should on thinking about what they must do.

25. The challenge is to guide the mind through or around all obstacles to accomplish the goal of divinity. This is the true and ultimate purpose of our reality.

26. Despite their loath to do so, humanity has always been dimly aware that they can influence their minds and direct their thoughts to realize any feat and construct any reality.

27. You are capable of instilling powerful and beneficial thoughts into your mind, but this can only be done by upgrading your belief to receive something greater.

28. Self-sufficiency and self-confidence are the inevitable results of a strong will, the intelligent application of methodology, and insistent diligence.

29. These self-actualizing beliefs can repair all physical and psychological impairments, replace weak ideals with strong ones, exchange ignorance for wisdom, and fortify the power and assurance of one's divine abilities.

30. Used judiciously, your mind can contribute a great deal to the success of humanity reaching their highest grade of refinement.

31. In every area of life, good judgment is necessary for favorable results. The effectiveness of success depends entirely upon subtle prudence.

32. All truths prevail by sheer force of being despite ignorance, indifference, or interest.

33. Your divine abilities are truly extraordinary, as they allow you to perform acts beyond the laws and forces of nature. It is in you to induce these abilities by anatomizing and mastering the presence of the mind and all phenomena.

34. If you exist but for one second there is in that single moment the most perplexing and extraordinary phenomenon. Very few will acquire the wisdom to take hold and persist.

35. All who accept and embrace the idea of achieving their state of divinity will excel and transcend beyond the evidence that binds humanity to the fateful nature of metaphysics.

36. All laws are merely commands imposed by superior forces upon inferior entities. The truly autonomous being is compelled by no existing law.

37. Let these propositions guide and enlighten you to develop the most conducive attributes.

38. No matter how great your achievements, how extensive your material possessions, or how noble your reputation, if you are not attentive to your personal health, physical condition, and psychological well-being, you are running the risk of losing it all.

39. Possessing the active force of a mind, you must reinforce your conscience, guide it by the ways of wisdom, and lead it along the true path.

40. The objects of thought produce interest, incite beliefs, and will lead you to those realities manifested by your desire to observe and encounter them in greater detail.

41. Believe in these doctrines and practice them incessantly. This way you will insure your transcendence and manifest divinity.

42. Believe this and you will discover your ultimate truth; God is with you, God is in you, you are the very essence of God, and you have the spirit of God. Indeed you are to assume this likeness and emulate these superlative qualities.

43. Avoid or escape those who are chaotic, violent, or overcome by misery. However, those who are competent and confident in their intellectual and spiritual aptitude should use their skills to relieve such individuals of these improper behaviors.

44. Pursue your desires but be mindful of your attachment to what belongs to the world.

45. Many things desired is merely the result of a mind without true intellectual qualities. Such individuals will always strive to fill the presence of their lives with material objects, for they cannot comprehend nor realize the massive power of self-contentment.

46. The objects of thought are the essential factors of reality and experience. Through them the assimilation of all ideals and creations are manifest.

47. Through your perception of these teachings you will examine your beliefs and determine their relevance to your purpose and ideals. Embrace what is most conducive to the ascension of your spirit.

48. Forge and customize your mind with the most edifying subjects and you will surely become that which you desire to be and achieve that which you aspire to achieve.

49. Not all are worthy of divine knowledge. However, those who do possess this power have a clear conscience, and indubitable faith. They are able to command the forces of life proficiently.

50. Protect your eyes and ears from all perversity and your spirit will be a holy temple for all to see the invigorating vitalities of life. Through this uncompromising stance, you will inherit the distinguished ideals of wisdom

THOUGHTS AND PERSPECTIVES

THOUGHTS AND PERSPECTIVES